D0118234

THE

OAT BRAN
Cookbook

THE
OAT
BRAN
Cookbook

Kitty and Lucian Maynard

RUTLEDGE HILL PRESS
Nashville, Tennessee

ALBANY COUNTY
PUBLIC LIBRARY
LARAMIE, WYOMING

WITHDRAWN

Copyright © 1989 Kitty E. Maynard and Lucian Maynard

All rights reserved. Written permission must be secured from the publisher to use or re-produce any part of this book, except for brief quotations in critical reviews or articles.

Published in Nashville, Tennessee, by Rutledge Hill Press, 513 Third Avenue South, Nashville, Tennessee 37210.

Typography by Bailey Typography, Inc., Nashville, Tennessee. Design by Harriette Bateman. Art by Tonya Pitkin, Studio III Productions.

Library of Congress Cataloging-in-Publication Data
Maynard, Kitty, 1955-
    The oat bran cookbook / Kitty and Lucian Maynard.
      p. cm.
    Includes index.
    ISBN 1-55853-016-9
    1. Cookery (Oat bran)   I. Maynard, Lucian, 1952- . II. Title.
TX809.O22M38 1989
641.6'313—dc19   89-5896
                                     CIP

Printed in the United States of America
  3 4 5 6 7 8—95 94 93 92 91 90 89

CONTENTS

Dedicated to the people of Jackson, Mississippi, and Lansing, Michigan, who participated in the National Lower Your Cholesterol Competition. You are leaders for the entire nation.

PREFACE

Now more than ever, Americans are becoming aware of their health needs and the various diets and foods available for good eating. More people are walking, jogging, and running today, and in many cities health clubs have had to close their memberships because they already are too full. Moreover, with so many people aware of the principles of healthy nutrition, grocers' shelves now contain numerous products that boast of having no cholesterol or less fat. Since this is a trend—and not a fad—it signifies America's movement toward becoming a healthier society.

In 1986 we began our personal research into the special needs of restricted diets and what people missed by following them. What we found was that, generally, we all are willing to give up our fast-foods and fat-riddled foods if we can replace them with alternatives that taste good. This has been made more pleasant by oat bran, which has a natural sweetness that satisfies as well as provides for nutritious eating. We also found that working with oat bran in cooking made for interesting eating, for it gave texture to foods without being grainy.

We have been using oat bran in our products at Miss Kitty's Pie in the Sky for well over a year and are pleased with the results. Numerous diabetics are thrilled to report that for the first time in their diabetic lives they can eat well and not feel deprived. They also report that sugar levels which have been so difficult to control are no longer a problem. We have received thanks from doctors and weight loss specialists, and our patrons have reported a decrease in cholesterol as well.

We are not so silly as to believe that we are the sole reason for these changes, but we know we have helped. At Miss Kitty's we encourage a diet high in complex carbohydrates, low in fats, and high in oat bran. We also encourage moderate exercise as a way to feel better and relieve stress. We are pleased at the results and will continue this program as long as our patrons continue to see wonderful results in their health.

The Oat Bran Cookbook has been written in response to the patrons of our shop and customers from across the country, many of whom have contacted us after hearing from friends and family members. We hope you, too, will make a place for oat bran in your—and your family's—future.

—Kitty and Lucian Maynard

THE

OAT BRAN
Cookbook

OAT BRAN:
AN INTRODUCTION

WHAT IS OAT BRAN?

Contrary to popular belief, oat bran has been around for a long time. It is not something new. The by-product of milling oats, oat bran is the outer husk or covering found on oat seeds. For many years, this husk has been removed as oats were processed for human consumption. For the most part, this "leftover" part of the oat has been put into pet food as a filler agent and has not been part of most people's daily diet.

All this began to change when, in 1977, a metabolic research team at the Veterans Administration hospital in Lexington, Kentucky, began its research. They were studying the effect of high fiber diets on diabetics, concentrating on whether a high fiber diet (one containing mixture of soluble and insoluble fibers) would help in controlling blood sugar and the need for insulins. Through these studies it was discovered that increasing fiber in the diet was effective in controlling blood glucose levels, as well as serum cholesterol levels.

The participants in the study at the Lexington Veterans Administration hospital ate 140 grams (approximately five bowls) of fiber daily. After many complained that eating such a large volume of fiber each day was too much, Dr. James W. Anderson (professor of medicine and of clinical nutrition at the University of Kentucky and chief of the endocrine-metabolic section of the Veterans Administration Medical Center in Lexington) began using oat bran solely, instead of the fifteen fibers used during his cholesterol and blood-sugar level study. The results of his studies show that a diet restricted in fat and cholesterol, and including 35 to 40 grams of oat bran daily, significantly decreases the level of LDL cholesterol (the harmful cholesterol) in the blood.*

*Based on research studies reported in "Plant Fiber: Carbohydrate and Lipid Metabolism," Anderson, J., and Chen, W., *American Journal of Clinical Nutrition,* 1979:43:346.

WHAT KIND OF FIBER IS OAT BRAN?

For years the public has been provided with information about bran. In almost all cases this bran was wheat bran (insoluble fiber). We have been told to eat fiber so we may increase roughage in our diets, thus possibly preventing colon cancer. This is done because insoluble fiber increases intestinal regularity; it is nature's laxative. Foods high in bulk travel quickly through the digestive system, giving little opportunity for carcinogens to come in contact with the gastrointestinal system.

Foods High in Insoluble Fiber (Foods followed by asterisk [*] are best when eaten with their skins.)

whole wheat flour
wheat bran
cabbage
young peas
green beans
broccoli
brussels sprouts
cucumber skins
peppers
apples*

carrots*
bran cereals
whole grains
mustard greens
beet root*
strawberries
eggplant
pears*
radishes

Oat bran is a water soluble fiber. This means that oat bran disperses easily in water and forms a gel-like substance during digestion. Oat bran fiber appears to slow the absorption of carbohydrates; thus it is useful in the diabetic's diet. Because of soluble fiber, oat bran controls the rise in blood sugar after meals. Soluble fiber also binds with bile acids, thereby decreasing fat absorption and lowering cholesterol levels; it coats the digestive tract.

Foods High in Soluble Fiber

oatmeal and other
   rolled oat products
dried beans
squash
apples
citrus fruits
cauliflower

green beans
cabbage
dried peas
carrots
strawberries
potatoes

WHAT FORM OF OAT BRAN IS BEST?

Oats come in many different forms: oat groats, steel-cut oats, old-fashioned rolled oats, quick rolled oats, and instant oats. These are just a few of the products with which we are the most familiar.

Oat Groats. When oats are harvested, they are in the kernel—or seed—form. This is the oat groat. The oat groat is the oat's natural state with its complete whole grain goodness. Oat groats have a sweet, nutty flavor and can be used in breads and muffins, with rice, or even cooked as a cereal. Found mainly in health food stores, oat groats should be cooked exactly according to the package instructions. It takes special care to cook them correctly.

Steel-Cut Oats. Also known as Irish or Scottish oats, steel-cut oats are oat groats that have been cut by a steel blade. They retain all their nutritional value, for they are not processed or heated. They are good for use in breads, muffins, pancakes, cookies, and soups and can be blended with other flours to add nutrition and oat fiber. You can cut your own oats by processing them with a steel blade in a food processor.

Old-fashioned Rolled Oats (or five-minute oats). We commonly refer to this as oatmeal. Oatmeal is derived from the oat groat and contains oat bran. There is almost no limit to the ways in which rolled oats can be used, and they cook quickly and easily in comparison to the oat groat.

Quick Rolled Oats (or minute oats). Quick rolled oats have been cut into pieces and processed to aid in quick preparation. As with old-fashioned oats, there is almost no limit to the ways in which they can be used.

Instant Oats. These are found on the grocery shelf in already-flavored, heat 'em up cereal packets. These oats are of lesser value for nutrition and bran and generally are not called for in the recipes in *The Oat Bran Cookbook.*

Oat Flour. This is a milled oat groat that contains the whole oat, oat bran included. Oat flour is useful for mixing with other flours (particularly whole wheat). It is useful in all recipes.

Oat Bran. While it is the best oat product available, it can be the most difficult to find. A finely ground product derived from the outer casing of the oat seed, oat bran is your best possible source of soluble fiber.

HOW MUCH IS THERAPEUTIC?

Figuring the amount of fiber needed each day can be difficult. Leading researchers such as Dr. James Anderson recommend that you include 35 to 50 grams of oat bran per day, but these figures tell you little about how much oat bran to include in each meal. As is the case with most issues of diet and health, a little common sense goes a long way as you plan to include oat bran in your daily diet.

One simple way to get oat bran into your diet is to include some form of it in every meal. For instance, have oat bran cereal for breakfast, a sandwich with oat bran bread for lunch, oat bran bread and a variety of vegetables for dinner, and an oat bran muffin as a snack. As unscientific as this sounds, by following this approach you will get a substantial amount of oat bran in your diet. Following this approach, you can then increase the amount of oat bran you eat each day as long as it does not cause bowel discomfort.

It is important to first consult your physician or diet counselor about your cholesterol levels. Take their advice regarding the amount of fiber needed in your diet, and then stick with their recommendations. By following the nutritional analysis provided with each recipe in *The Oat Bran Cookbook,* you can carefully monitor the amounts of all key elements of your diet.

WHAT IS CHOLESTEROL?

Cholesterol is a natural fat that normally circulates within the blood stream. When too much cholesterol is consumed, however, a build-up occurs within the blood vessels. If steps are not taken to correct the amount of cholesterol eaten (and stored), eventually a blockage will occur, with its disastrous results.

What are the normal ranges for cholesterol? The following chart provides information based on age alone as suggested by one major medical facility; neither sex nor other factors normally taken into account in medical research are included. Since it is possible that these levels will vary according to new developments in research and testing, it is important that you consult with your personal physician or diet counselor to determine your ideal range.

Age	Normal Level	Critical Level
0–19 years	70–170	Less than 30 Greater than 185
19–29 years	120–200	Less than 30 Greater than 220
29–39 years	120–220	Less than 30 Greater than 240
39–127 years*	120–240	Less than 30 Greater than 260

*Optimistic medical society figures life span through age 127!

WHAT TO AVOID AND WHAT TO DO

1. Avoid foods that are high in sugar. Be careful of "disguised" sugar as well, such as fructose, honey, and corn syrup.

2 Avoid visible and invisible fats. Read labels and pay attention to the amount of fat. Remember, the less saturated fat the better the product is for you. Restrict your consumption of whole eggs and hard cheeses. Use skim milk instead of whole milk.

3. Avoid salt. This includes meats that are salt cured.

4. Limit the amount of red meat you eat. Limiting yourself to eating red meat twice a week is a good rule to follow. Eat white meats such as fish and poultry. Bake, grill, roast, stew, or sauté your meats. Never fry or deep fry them.

5. Use margarines and oils low in saturated fat. Pay attention to the amounts of saturated fat, especially in margarine. The softer the margarine, the less fat within. Canola oil (Puritan), safflower oil, and vegetable oils are good, but you still must pay attention to the saturated fats. Remember that palm oil and coconut oil are high in saturated fats and should be avoided.

6. Eat vegetables, the fresher the better. Fresh vegetables can be very tasty when eaten steamed or raw; canned vegetables generally include added salts. Frozen vegetables can also be useful during the winter months when fresh vegetables are not available. By increasing the amount of vegetables in your diet, you will increase the amount of soluble and insoluble fiber.

BALANCE IS THE ANSWER

Every significant change in your life involves commitment, so begin by committing yourself to a healthy diet. It might help if you begin a diary that you update daily to include all meals and snacks. By keeping this daily diary you help reinforce in your own mind your allowances per day.

Exercise must be the second component of your new diet. Balance means balanced meals and balanced exercise. It is not necessary to run in marathon races to get the exercise you need. Begin by finding what exercises you enjoy the most. Walk, ski, run, swim, bike, or whatever you enjoy and helps you relax. If you enjoy the exercise, you will continue it. If you have not been exercising, begin with ten minutes, twice a day. Build your exercise program to 30 minutes twice a day for maximum benefits.

A FINAL WORD

You will note that several recipes in this volume do not include oat bran in their ingredients. However, all of the recipes do contain soluble fiber. When you do not find oat bran in a recipe, the recipe will contain at least one of the foods listed under "Foods High in Soluble Fiber" on page thirteen. Our reason for including these recipes is to provide a variety of ways for you to eat soluble fiber.

BEVERAGES

⁘ ⁘ ⁘

Curried Tomato-Celery Drink

1 46-ounce can tomato juice
1 teaspoon curry powder
½ cup celery puree
Dash Tabasco

Combine ½ cup of the tomato juice and the curry powder in a small bowl. Stir to blend well. Add the celery juice, Tabasco and remaining tomato juice and heat to boiling. Refrigerate. Serve chilled.
    Serves 6.

Per serving: 44 calories, 3% of calories from fat, 3 gm fiber, 0.00 mg cholesterol, 864 mg sodium, 0.17 gm fat, 0.03 gm saturated fat, 0.07 gm polyunsaturated fat, 0.03 gm monounsaturated fat.

Tomato Frappé

1 tablespoon cholesterol-
  free margarine
3 tablespoons finely
  chopped onion
1 tablespoon lemon juice
⅛ teaspoon Worcestershire
  sauce
⅛ teaspoon Tabasco sauce
4 cups tomato juice
1 vegetable bouillon cube or
  1 teaspoon instant bouillon granules
Lemon wedges

Melt the margarine and sauté the chopped onion until tender and translucent. Place the sautéed onion, lemon juice, Worcestershire, Tabasco, and tomato juice in a blender. Blend for 1 minute or until smooth. Add the vegetable bouillon and blend again until dissolved. Pour into a metal baking pan and freeze. Half an hour before needed, remove the tomato mix from the freezer. Thaw just enough to break into chunks. Place in a food processor and blend until smooth. Don't let it melt. Serve in sherbet glasses with a lemon wedge and straws.
Serves 6.

Per serving: 49 calories, 33% of calories from fat, 2 gm fiber, 0.00 mg cholesterol, 755 mg sodium, 2.05 gm fat, 0.36 gm saturated fat, 0.87 gm polyunsaturated fat, 0.70 gm monounsaturated fat.

Tomato Twist

10 ounces stewed tomatoes,
  fresh or canned
2 tablespoons lemon juice
2 tablespoons lime juice
1 teaspoon Worcestershire
  sauce
4 drops Tabasco sauce
1 cup cold water
Lime slices

Combine the stewed tomatoes, juices, and seasonings in a blender and blend for 30 seconds on medium speed. Add the cold water, stir, and pour into old-fashioned glasses filled with crushed ice. Garnish each with a slice of lime.
  Serves 6.

Per serving: 10 calories, 9% of calories from fat, 0.38 gm fiber, 0.00 mg cholesterol, 84.6 mg sodium, 0.12 gm fat, 0.02 gm saturated fat, 0.05 gm polyunsaturated fat, 0.02 gm monounsaturated fat.

Apple-Strawberry Cream Shake

2 apples, peeled and pureed
1 cup ripe fresh strawberries
½ cup lowfat vanilla yogurt

Combine the pureed apples, strawberries, and yogurt in a food processor. Puree until completely combined and thick. Pour into 4 wine glasses and top each with a ripe strawberry.
  Serves 4.

Per serving: 91.5 calories, 12% of calories from fat, 2.46 gm fiber, 3.50 mg cholesterol, 40.8 mg sodium, 1.26 gm fat 0.62 gm saturated fat, 0.17 gm polyunsaturated fat, 0.27 gm monounsaturated fat.

SALADS

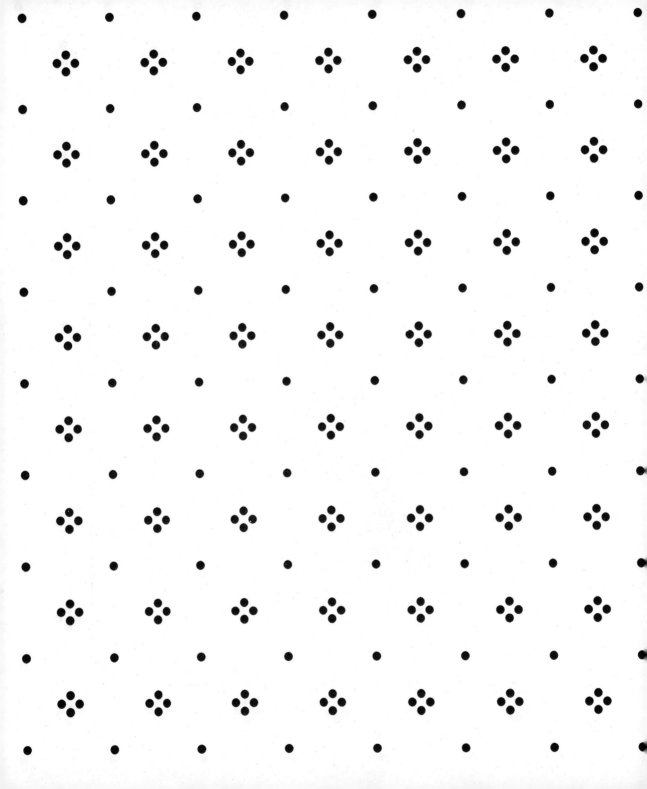

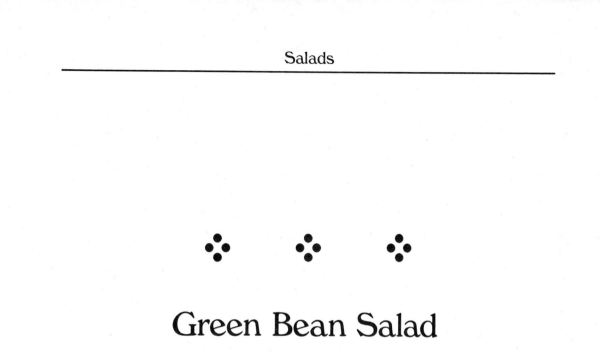

Green Bean Salad

1 10-ounce package frozen
  cut green beans
¾ cup vegetable oil
¼ cup water
¼ cup white wine vinegar
  with tarragon
1 teaspoon sugar
Dash pepper
⅛ teaspoon paprika
½ teaspoon dry mustard
½ teaspoon Worcestershire
  sauce
1 clove garlic, minced (optional)
1 tablespoon finely chopped
  onion
2 teaspoons finely chopped
  parsley

Cook the green beans as directed on the package; drain and set aside. Combine the remaining ingredients; blend well. Pour the marinade mixture over the green beans and refrigerate for a few hours. When ready to serve, drain the green beans and serve on salad plates.
  Serves 4.

Per serving: 386 calories, 93% of calories from fat, 1.20 gm fiber, 0.00 mg cholesterol, 15.4 mg sodium, 41 gm fat, 5.96 gm saturated fat, 15.4 gm polyunsaturated fat, 17.6 gm monounsaturated fat.

Wild Rice Salad

1 6-ounce package wild rice mix
½ cup reduced calorie mayonnaise
⅓ cup plain lowfat yogurt
1 cup sliced celery
1 cup cubed tomato
½ cup diced cucumber
2 tablespoons chopped parsley
⅛ teaspoon Mrs. Dash seasoning
⅛ teaspoon pepper

Cook the rice as directed on the package, omitting margarine. Cool. Toss lightly with the remaining ingredients. Cover and chill.
Serves 6.

Per serving: 226 calories, 27% of calories from fat, 4.64 gm fiber, 7.77 mg cholesterol, 6.11 mg sodium, 6.72 gm fat, 0.23 gm saturated fat, 0.10 gm polyunsaturated fat, 0.30 gm monounsaturated fat.

Mellow Ambrosia

2 medium oranges, peeled and diced
1 small banana, sliced
¼ cup orange juice
1 tablespoon wheat germ
1 tablespoon toasted oat bran

Combine the fruits and juice, and portion into dessert dishes. Sprinkle with wheat germ and oat bran.
Serves 4.

Per serving: 76 calories, 6% of calories from fat, 2 gm fiber, 0.00 mg cholesterol, 0.49 mg sodium, 0.54 gm fat, 0.10 gm saturated fat, 0.16 gm polyunsaturated fat, 0.06 gm monounsaturated fat.

Orange-Pineapple Salad

1 16-ounce can mandarin oranges
1 16-ounce can crushed unsweetened pineapple

• • •

1 6-ounce package sugarfree orange gelatin
1 carrot, finely grated

• • •

Dash cinnamon
2 tablespoons plain lowfat yogurt
1 8-ounce carton nonfat cottage cheese

Drain the juices from the oranges and pineapple into a saucepan and bring to a boil. Remove from the heat. Mix in the gelatin, stirring until dissolved. When the gelatin has cooled, stir in the carrot, fruits, cinnamon, yogurt, and cottage cheese. Refrigerate overnight before serving.
  Serves 8.

Per serving: 164 calories, 3% of calories from fat, 0.68 gm fiber, 2.59 mg cholesterol, 149 mg sodium, 0.67 gm fat, 0.39 saturated fat, 0.04 gm polyunsaturated fat, 0.18 gm monounsaturated fat.

Waldorf Salad

2 cups diced unpeeled apple
1 cup diced celery
½ cup seedless grapes, halved
¼ cup raisins
1 teaspoon lemon juice
¼ cup chopped walnuts
¼ cup nonfat vanilla yogurt
Lettuce leaves
¼ cup oat bran

Toss together the apples, celery, grapes, and raisins in a medium bowl. Add the lemon juice and walnuts. Stir in the yogurt and spoon onto lettuce leaves on plates. Sprinkle the top of the salads with the oat bran.
  Serves 6.

Per serving: 85 calories, 22% of calories from fat, 3 gm fiber, 0.17 mg cholesterol, 25.8 mg sodium, 2.38 gm fat, 0.17 gm saturated fat, 1.31 gm polyunsaturated fat, 0.44 gm monounsaturated fat.

SOUPS

❖   ❖   ❖

Beef Stew

2 pounds stewing beef
2 medium onions, sliced
1 green pepper, chopped

¾ cup pureed whole
  tomatoes
¾ cup water
¼ teaspoon dried basil
  leaves
¼ teaspoon dried marjoram
⅛ teaspoon pepper
1 tablespoon Wor-
  cestershire sauce
1 cup diced green beans
2 medium potatoes, diced
2 medium carrots, sliced
1 medium zucchini, diced
2 stalks celery, chopped

Combine the stewing beef, onion, and green pepper together in a large skillet. Cook until the meat is brown and the vegetables are tender. Transfer to a Dutch oven and add the remaining ingredients. Bake at 350° for 1 hour or until the vegetables are tender. This can be served over wild rice.
　Serves 8.

Per serving: 472 calories, 59% of calories from fat, 2.57 gm fiber, 104 mg cholesterol, 199 mg sodium, 31 gm fat, 12.7 gm saturated fat, 1.27 gm polyunsaturated fat, 13.6 gm monounsaturated fat.

Family Style Chili

1 cup chopped onion
1 cup diced green pepper
2 pounds ground chuck, lean
½ cup cholesterol-free margarine
2 cloves garlic, minced
3 tablespoons chili powder
1½ teaspoons paprika
3 whole cloves
4 cups tomatoes, cooked and skinned
1 15-ounce can kidney beans
1 cup cooked brown rice

Brown the onion, green pepper and ground chuck in the margarine. Add the garlic, seasonings, and tomatoes. Cover and cook over low heat for about 1 hour. Add the kidney beans and brown rice during the last 15 minutes of cooking time.

Serves 10.

Per serving: 403 calories, 55% of calories from fat, 4 gm fiber, 75.8 mg cholesterol, 338 mg sodium, 24.6 gm fat, 7.43 gm saturated fat, 4.63 gm polyunsaturated fat, 9.77 gm monounsaturated fat.

Hot Hot Gumbo

⅓ cup all-purpose flour
⅓ cup oat bran
Pepper and paprika to taste
4 chicken breasts, skinned
    and boned
3 tablespoons safflower oil

•   •   •

1 cup chopped onion
1 cup chopped green pep-
    per
1 28-ounce can tomatoes,
    skinned
2 pounds okra, sliced
8 drops Tabasco sauce

•   •   •

4 cups cooked wild rice
Chopped green onion and/
    or chopped fresh parsley

Combine the flour, oat bran, pepper, and paprika. Dredge the chicken in this mixture, then brown in hot oil in a large skillet, turning to brown all sides. Remove and place in a baking dish. Bake at 350° for 20 minutes. Sauté the onion and green pepper in the oil left in the skillet. Stir until limp but not brown. Add the tomatoes, okra, and Tabasco and cook until tender. Place the chicken on a bed of rice and cover with the tomato and okra mix. Garnish with chopped green onion and parsley.
    Serves 8.

Per serving: 392 calories, 22% of calories from fat, 6.35 gm fiber, 73 mg cholesterol, 230.5 mg sodium, 9.5 gm fat, 1.46 gm saturated fat, 4.68 gm polyunsaturated fat, 1.77 gm monounsaturated fat.

Thick Cabbage Chowder

4 cups coarsely shredded
   cabbage
2 cups sliced carrots
3 cups diced potatoes
½ teaspoon sugar
¼ teaspoon pepper
3 cups water
4 cups milk, scalded
2 tablespoons cholesterol-
   free margarine
¾ cup oat bran

Cook the vegetables and seasonings in water until tender. Add the scalded milk and margarine. Stir in the oat bran and cook but do not boil for an additional 5 minutes.
   Serves 8.

Per serving: 196 calories, 17% of calories from fat, 4.35 gm fiber, 2 mg cholesterol, 137 mg sodium, 3.9 gm fat, 0.68 gm saturated fat, 1.34 gm polyunsaturated fat, 1.08 gm monounsaturated fat.

Clam Chowder

½ cup chopped mushrooms
1 cup chopped celery
1 cup chopped onion
¼ cup cholesterol-free margarine

1 quart boiling water
1 cup finely diced carrots
1 cup diced potatoes

2 tablespoons cholesterol-
   free margarine
¼ cup all-purpose flour
¼ cup oat bran
1 gallon skim milk

Sauté the mushrooms, celery, and onion in ¼ cup of margarine in a large heavy saucepan. Add the water, carrots and potatoes. Simmer for 20 minutes, or until the vegetables are tender.
   While the vegetables are simmering, make a thin white sauce by melting 2 tablespoons of margarine in a saucepan over medium heat. Stir in the flour and oat bran, and mix well. Add in the skim milk and stir occasionally until thickened. Set aside. When the vegetables are tender, add the clams with their juice, pimientos, white wine, and the white sauce. Cook 10 minutes longer. Serve piping hot.
   Serves 8 to 12.

2 6½-ounce cans chopped
clams, including juice
1 tablespoon chopped pi-
mientos
¼ cup dry white wine

Per serving: 332 calories, 28% of calories from fat, 1.95 gm fiber, 36.7 mg cholesterol, 419 mg sodium, 10.4 gm fat, 2.18 gm saturated fat, 3.78 gm polyunsaturated fat, 3.28 gm monounsaturated fat.

Vegetable Chowder

1 large potato, peeled and
cubed

•   •   •

3 tablespoons cholesterol-
free margarine
¼ cup all-purpose flour
3 tablespoons oat bran
2 pints unsalted chicken
broth

•   •   •

1 large onion, minced
2 ribs celery, minced
1 large carrot, finely
chopped
Cholesterol-free margarine

•   •   •

½ cup broccoli flowerets
½ cup cauliflower flowerets

•   •   •

1 pint skim milk
1 clove garlic, minced
Pepper to taste

Place the potatoes in cold water and bring to a boil. Cook until tender. Cool and reserve. Melt the margarine and add the flour and oat bran slowly to make a roux. Bring the chicken stock to a boil in a stock pot and thicken with the roux. Return to a boil, and reduce to a simmer.

Sauté the onion, celery, and carrots in margarine for 10 minutes, stirring constantly. Add the broccoli and cauliflower for the last 5 minutes of cooking. Strain the chicken stock into this mixture and add the potatoes. Bring to a boil and simmer until the vegetables are done. Add skim milk, garlic, and pepper, and gently return to just boiling. Serve at once.

Serves 8 to 10.

Per serving: 129 calories, 37% of calories from fat, 2.01 gm fiber, 1.0 mg cholesterol, 131 mg sodium, 5.48 gm fat, 0.84 gm saturated fat, 1.9 gm polyunsaturated fat, 1.56 gm monounsaturated fat.

Cream of Chicken and Wild Rice Soup

½ cup uncooked wild rice
1 tablespoon soy sauce
1½ cups water

•   •

¼ cup cholesterol-free margarine
3 large cloves garlic, minced
1 medium onion, chopped
2 carrots, finely diced
6 stalks asparagus, finely diced

•   •   •

½ cup all-purpose flour
¼ cup oat bran

•   •   •

5 cups chicken stock
1 cup chopped chicken breast
½ teaspoon thyme
1 bay leaf
Minced parsley
Pepper to taste

•   •   •

4 cups skim milk

Cook the wild rice with the soy sauce and water in a covered pan. Melt the margarine in a large saucepan and sauté the garlic and onion until tender. Add the carrots and asparagus, and cook until tender. Stir in the flour and cereal, and cook over low heat for approximately 10 minutes, stirring frequently. Whisk in the chicken stock, blending until smooth. Add the chicken and seasonings. Slowly add the skim milk and simmer for 20 minutes. Fold in the prepared rice and serve.

Serves 10.

Per serving: 176 calories, 33% of calories from fat, 1.60 gm fiber, 14.8 mg cholesterol, 620 mg sodium, 6.35 gm fat, 1.28 gm saturated fat, 2.27 gm polyunsaturated fat, 2.17 gm monounsaturated fat.

Meatball Soup

1 pound lean ground chuck
¼ cup oat bran
1 tablespoon parsley
1 tablespoon minced onion
¼ teaspoon oregano
Pepper to taste

•   •   •

1 quart sodium-free chicken
   broth
1 pound fresh cut or frozen
   spinach

•   •   •

1 cup tortellini, cholesterol-
   free if available

Combine the first 6 ingredients and shape into small meatballs. Brown in the oven. Drain the meatballs and add to the chicken broth along with the spinach. Simmer for 10 minutes. Cook and drain the tortellini. Add to the soup just before serving.
   Serves 10.

Per serving: 168 calories, 45% of calories from fat, 1.47 gm fiber, 42.9 mg cholesterol, 92.3 mg sodium, 8.49 gm fat, 2.92 gm saturated fat, 0.32 gm polyunsaturated fat, 3.25 gm monounsaturated fat.

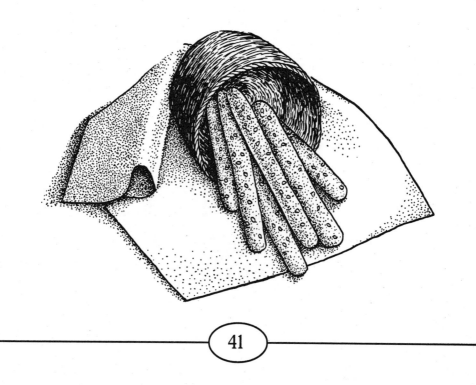

Gingered Carrot Soup

1 pound carrots, peeled and
  sliced
1 pound tomatoes
2 large onions, chopped
1 clove garlic, chopped
½ cup unsweetened orange
  juice
2 tablespoons chopped parsley
2 teaspoons seasoned salt
  substitute
Pepper to taste
1 teaspoon ginger

½ cup skim milk
¼ cup cholesterol-free margarine
3 tablespoons oat bran

Place the carrots, tomatoes, onions, garlic, orange juice, parsley, seasoned salt, pepper, and ginger in a large stock pot. Cover with water and cook until tender. Drain and puree in a food processor. Return to the pot and add the skim milk, margarine, and oat bran. Stir and simmer for approximately 10 minutes more. This can be served in a cleaned out pumpkin and heated in a warm oven for about 5 minutes.

Serves 8.

Per serving: 115 calories, 46% of calories from fat, 3.46 gm fiber, 0.25 mg cholesterol, 111 mg sodium, 6.23 gm fat, 1.05 gm saturated fat, 2.59 gm polyunsaturated fat, 2.07 gm monounsaturated fat.

Creamy Cucumber Soup

2 medium cucumbers,
   peeled and sliced (about 3
   cups)
1 cup water
¼ cup sliced onion
¼ teaspoon salt substitute
⅛ teaspoon pepper
¼ cup all-purpose flour
¼ cup oat bran
2 cups unsalted chicken
   broth, divided
¼ teaspoon ground cloves
¼ teaspoon paprika
1 cup plain nonfat yogurt,
   chilled
1 tablespoon finely chopped
   dill

Combine the cucumber slices with water, onion, salt substitute, and pepper in a 2 quart saucepan. Cook until very soft, approximately 30 minutes. Put through a strainer or blend in a food processor until smooth. Set aside. Combine the flour and oat bran with ½ of the chicken broth in the same saucepan. Stir until smooth. Gradually add the remaining chicken broth and blend well. Add the puree, cloves, and paprika. Stir over medium heat until the mixture begins to simmer. Reduce the heat to a simmer and cook for an additional 2 minutes. Do not boil. Remove from the heat and refrigerate. Just before serving, stir in the yogurt and dill. Serve very cold in chilled bowls.
   Serves 4.

Per serving: 125 calories, 11% of calories from fat, 3.52 gm fiber, 1.5 mg cholesterol, 435 mg sodium, 1.51 gm fat, 0.34 gm saturated fat, 0.25 gm polyunsaturated fat, 0.36 gm monounsaturated fat.

Cold Weather Soup

6 cups water
6 cubes reduced-sodium
  chicken bouillon
2 medium carrots, pared
  and diced
1 cup lima beans
1 large potato, pared and
  diced
1 cup shredded cabbage
2 medium ribs celery,
  chopped
1 medium onion, chopped
1 small white turnip,
  chopped
⅛ teaspoon nutmeg
⅛ teaspoon pepper
¼ cup dry white wine

Bring the water and bouillon cubes to a boil in a 3 quart saucepot. Add the carrots, lima beans, potato, cabbage, celery, onion, turnip, nutmeg, and pepper. Return to a boil, lower the temperature to a simmer, and add the wine. Simmer until the vegetables are tender, about 25 minutes.
    Serves 6.

Per serving: 91.8 calories, 4% of calories from fat, 3.78 gm fiber, 0.14 mg cholesterol, 916 mg sodium, 0.42 gm fat, 0.12 gm saturated fat, 0.14 gm polyunsaturated fat, 0.08 gm monounsaturated fat.

Fall Harvest Soup

1 2-pound butternut squash,
   peeled and cubed
4 cups chicken stock

. . .

2 cooking apples, peeled
   and quartered

. . .

2 tablespoons lemon juice
Pepper to taste
¼ teaspoon nutmeg
Mrs. Dash seasoning to
   taste
1 cup skim milk
½ cup oat bran

Cook the squash in chicken stock until tender, about 10 minutes. Add the apples and cook until soft. Drain, reserving the liquid. Puree the squash and apples in a food processor. Reheat with the reserved stock, and add the lemon juice and seasonings. Stir in the milk and oat bran. Heat thoroughly, but do not boil.

   Serves 6 to 8.

Per serving: 151 calories, 10% of calories from fat, 4.71 gm fiber, 1.33 mg cholesterol, 544 mg sodium, 1.80 gm fat, 0.38 gm saturated fat, 0.30 gm polyunsaturated fat, 0.46 gm monounsaturated fat.

Hearty Potato Soup

1 tablespoon cholesterol-
  free margarine
1 medium onion, chopped
⅓ cup chopped green pep-
  per
1 clove garlic, minced

   .   .   .

½ cup oat bran
2 carrots, sliced
4 small potatoes, peeled
  and diced
¼ cup diced celery
½ cup chicken broth
2½ cups skim milk
1½ teaspoons curry powder
Pinch salt and pepper
Pinch nutmeg

Melt the margarine in a saucepan and sauté the onion, green pepper, and garlic for 3 to 4 minutes. Add the remaining ingredients and stir. Simmer for 35 to 45 minutes or until the potatoes are tender. Pour into a blender or processor and puree. Pour back into the saucepan and heat to serving temperature.
   Serves 8.

Per serving: 135 calories, 14% of calories from fat, 2.49 gm fiber, 1.31 mg cholesterol, 169 mg sodium, 2.24 gm fat, 0.40 gm saturated fat, 0.73 gm polyunsaturated fat, 0.59 gm monounsaturated fat.

Summer Strawberry and Burgundy Soup

3 pints strawberries,
  washed and hulled
1 cup water

   .   .   .

¼ cup sugar
¼ cup oat bran
2 cups burgundy

Quarter the strawberries and cook in water for 10 minutes. Combine the sugar and oat bran in a separate saucepan. Stir in the wine and orange juice. Stir or whisk until the mixture boils, approximately 10 minutes. Remove from heat immediately and add the strawberries. Cool. Puree

2 cups unsweetened orange
juice

• • •

3 cups plain nonfat yogurt
1 cup skim milk

• • •

Sliced strawberries for garnish
Mint leaves for garnish

the strawberry mixture in a blender or food processor and add the yogurt and skim milk. Chill.
Serve garnished with strawberries and mint
leaves.
Serves 8.

Per serving: 194 calories, 4% of calories from fat, 3.30 gm
fiber, 2.00 mg cholesterol, 86.4 mg sodium, 0.95 gm fat, 0.17
gm saturated fat, 0.24 gm polyunsaturated fat, 0.59 gm
monounsaturated fat.

Zucchini Soup

8 small zucchini, sliced
1 cup water
1 small onion, minced
2 tablespoons reduced-
sodium chicken bouillon
granules
1 teaspoon fresh parsley

• • •

¼ cup rolled oats
3 cups skim milk
3 tablespoons cholesterol-
free margarine
2 tablespoons reduced-
sodium chicken bouillon
granules

Cook the zucchini in water with the onion, 2
tablespoons of chicken bouillon granules, and
parsley until tender.
Place the rolled oats in a small bowl. Gradually
stir in a small amount of the skim milk. Combine
in a saucepan the oat mixture, the remaining
milk, margarine, and 2 tablespoons of chicken
bouillon granules. Simmer over medium heat,
stirring occasionally, until the mixture has thickened. Puree the zucchini mixture in a blender
and add it to the oat mixture. Serve hot.
Serves 12.

Per serving: 69.3 calories, 46% of calories from fat, 0.66
gm fiber, 1.00 mg cholesterol, 88.8 mg sodium, 3.64 gm fat,
0.58 gm saturated fat, 1.26 gm polyunsaturated fat, 1.05 gm
monounsaturated fat.

BREADS

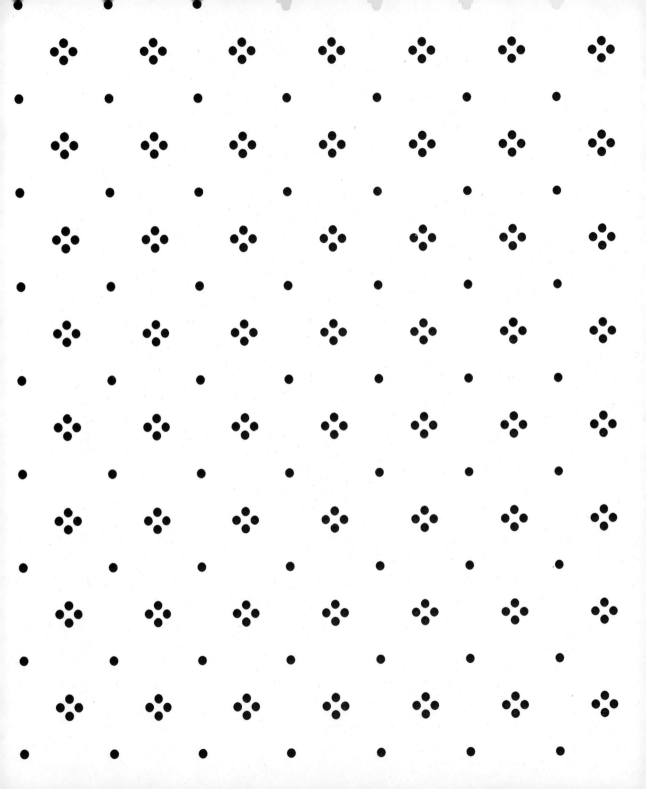

Apricot Bread

1¼ cups all-purpose flour
½ cup brown sugar
1 teaspoon baking powder
½ teaspoon baking soda
⅔ cup water
½ cup chopped dried apri-
   cots
¾ cup oat bran
½ cup orange juice
4 egg whites
¼ cup vegetable oil
1 teaspoon vanilla extract
¼ cup chopped walnuts

Combine the flour, brown sugar, baking powder, and baking soda in a medium bowl. In a separate bowl, combine the water with the dried apricots, oat bran, orange juice, egg whites, oil, and vanilla. Add the dry ingredients, stirring until combined. Stir in the walnuts. Spoon into a greased loaf pan. Bake at 375° for 20 minutes or until done.

Makes 1 loaf, or 15 servings.

Per serving: 179 calories, 32% of calories from fat, 1.70 gm fiber, 0.00 mg cholesterol, 83.0 mg sodium, 6.64 gm fat, 0.83 gm saturated fat, 2.70 gm polyunsaturated fat, 2.32 gm monounsaturated fat.

Blackberry-Zucchini Bread

¼ cup cholesterol-free oil
½ cup sugar
3 egg whites
1 tablespoon freshly grated
   orange rind
½ cup orange juice
1½ cups whole wheat flour
1½ cups oat bran
1 teaspoon baking soda
2 teaspoons baking powder
1 16-ounce can blackberries
   packed in water or 1
   package of frozen blackberries
1½ cups finely shredded
   zucchini

Combine all of the ingredients except the berries and zucchini. Fold in the drained berries and zucchini just until blended. Turn into a greased loaf pan and bake at 350° for 1½ hours (check after the first 45 minutes. If necessary, cover with aluminum foil to prevent browning too quickly).

Makes 1 loaf, or 15 servings.

Per serving: 152 calories, 25% of calories from fat, 4.53 gm fiber, 0.00 mg cholesterol, 111 mg sodium, 4.60 gm fat, 0.58 gm saturated fat, 1.39 gm polyunsaturated fat, 1.57 gm monounsaturated fat.

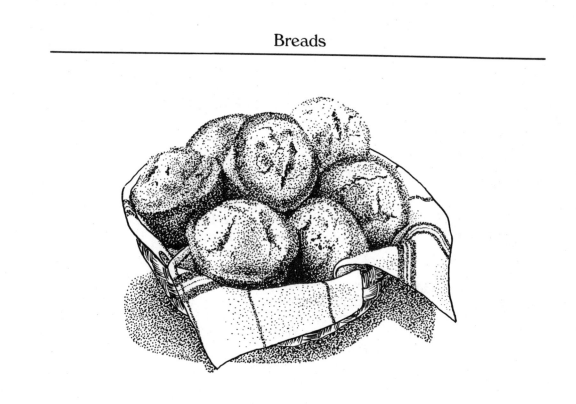

Blueberry-Banana Muffins

1 cup whole wheat flour
1 cup oat bran
1 teaspoon baking soda
2 teaspoons baking powder
½ teaspoon cinnamon
½ cup rolled oats
½ cup cholesterol-free oil
4 tablespoons sugar
1 egg white
1 tablespoon lemon juice
½ cup 100% pure un-
*   sweetened orange juice*
2 whole bananas, mashed
1 cup frozen blueberries

Combine all of the ingredients except the bananas and berries. Blend well. Gently fold in the bananas and blueberries using a wooden spoon. Spoon into greased muffin tins. Bake at 350° for 20 minutes.
   Makes 12 muffins.

Per serving: 195 calories, 44% of calories from fat, 3.25 gm fiber, 0.00 mg cholesterol, 130 mg sodium, 10.20 gm fat, 1.40 gm saturated fat, 3.44 gm polyunsaturated fat, 3.92 gm monounsaturated fat.

Buttermilk Bread

3 cups fine stone ground
  whole wheat flour
1 cup rye flour
1 cup rolled oats
¾ cup oat bran
1 quart lowfat buttermilk
2 tablespoons light brown
  sugar
1 tablespoon dark molasses
1 cup vegetable oil
2 ¼-ounce packages active
  dry yeast

Combine the flours, oats, and oat bran in a large bowl and set aside. Heat the buttermilk to lukewarm, not hot. Pour into a large bowl and add the sugar, molasses, and oil. Stir until dissolved. Add the yeast to 1 cup of the flour mixture, and stir into the liquid mixture. Let the dough rest for 12 minutes. (This step is important for it will give you the soft bread texture.) Add the remaining flour mixture and form a bread dough. The bread is ready to be kneaded when it is of a sticky but not wet consistency. Allow the dough to rise, punch down, and form into 2 loaves. Let the loaves rise for 1 hour or until double in bulk. Bake at 350° for 40 to 50 minutes.

Makes 2 loaves, or 30 servings.

Per serving: 114 calories, 60% of calories from fat, 0.83 gm fiber, 1.20 mg cholesterol, 34.8 mg sodium, 7.98 gm fat, 1.25 gm saturated fat, 2.74 gm polyunsaturated fat, 3.20 gm monounsaturated fat.

Oat Bran Bread

2½ cups boiling water
½ cup cholesterol-free margarine
¼ cup honey
2 ¼-ounce packages active
dry yeast
1¾ cups oat bran
1 cup chopped nuts
2 eggs
6 cups whole wheat flour

Combine the boiling water, margarine, and honey in a bowl. Cool to lukewarm. Combine the yeast with the oat bran and nuts, and mix well. Whisk into the lukewarm liquid. Add the eggs and mix well. Add the flour, and mix well by hand. This will make a stiff dough. Turn out onto a floured surface and knead for approximately 10 minutes or until smooth in texture. Place in an oiled bowl, cover, and let rise until double in bulk, approximately 1 hour. Punch down and form into 2 loaves. Place in loaf pans and allow to double in size. Bake at 375° for 30 to 35 minutes or until golden brown. Cool for at least 1 hour before slicing.

Makes 2 loaves, or 30 servings.

Per serving: 164 calories, 34% of calories from fat, 3.78 gm fiber, 18.3 mg cholesterol, 46.6 mg sodium, 6.66 gm fat, 0.94 gm saturated fat, 2.93 gm polyunsaturated fat, 1.79 gm monounsaturated fat.

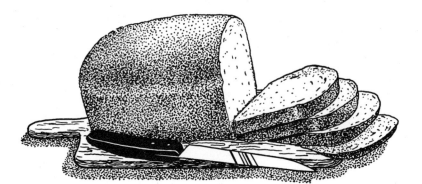

Oat Bran-Banana Bread

½ cup sorghum
⅓ cup vegetable oil
⅓ cup orange juice
1½ teaspoons vanilla extract
⅓ cup oat bran
2 medium bananas, mashed
1¼ teaspoons baking powder
½ teaspoon baking soda
1¾ cups all-purpose flour
1 teaspoon cinnamon
4 egg whites
¼ cup chopped nuts (optional)

Combine the sorghum and oil in a bowl. Add the orange juice, vanilla, oat bran, and bananas. Combine the dry ingredients in a separate bowl. Add dry ingredients to the sorghum mixture. Whip the egg whites until stiff. Gently fold the egg whites into the batter. Add the nuts. Spoon into a greased loaf pan. Bake at 350° for 1 hour or until golden brown and a knife inserted in the center comes out clean.

Makes 1 loaf, or 15 servings.

Per serving: 160 calories, 35% of calories from fat, 1.10 gm fiber, 0.00 mg cholesterol, 79.2 mg sodium, 6.37 gm fat, 0.87 gm saturated fat, 2.60 gm polyunsaturated fat, 2.36 gm monounsaturated fat.

Whole Wheat Banana Bread

¾ cup oat bran
¾ cup unsweetened orange juice

2 ripe bananas, mashed
3 tablespoons honey

Combine the first two ingredients, set aside, and allow to soak for 30 minutes.

Combine the mashed bananas, honey, oil, vanilla, and beaten egg whites. Stir in the orange juice mixture. Combine the remaining ingredients and stir into the banana mixture. Pour

½ cup vegetable oil
1 teaspoon vanilla extract
2 egg whites, beaten until fluffy
1½ cups whole wheat pastry flour
1 tablespoon baking powder
½ teaspoon cinnamon
½ cup chopped pecans

batter into a greased bread pan or 12 muffin tins. Bake at 350° for 1 hour for bread and for 20 minutes for muffins.

Makes 1 loaf, or 15 servings.

Per serving: 179 calories, 49% of calories from fat, 2.92 gm fiber, 0.00 mg cholesterol, 75.3 mg sodium, 10.3 gm fat, 1.33 gm saturated fat, 3.36 gm polyunsaturated fat, 4.65 gm monounsaturated fat.

Apple-Raisin Muffins

2 cups all-purpose flour
1 cup oat bran
2 teaspoons baking powder
½ teaspoon baking soda
1 teaspoon cinnamon
1 tablespoon sugar
2 egg whites
3 tablespoons cholesterol-free oil
½ cup apple juice
1 cup unsweetened applesauce
½ cup raisins
¼ cup chopped walnuts

Mix all of the ingredients together and pour into greased muffin tins. Bake at 350° for 20 minutes.

Makes 12 muffins.

Per serving: 183 calories, 27% of calories from fat, 2.50 gm fiber, 0.00 mg cholesterol, 101 mg sodium, 5.67 gm fat, 0.68 gm saturated fat, 2.28 gm polyunsaturated fat, 1.82 gm monounsaturated fat.

Apricot Muffins

Batter:
2 cups oat bran
¼ cup Miller's bran
½ cup whole wheat flour
2½ teaspoons baking powder
½ teaspoon cinnamon
¾ cup diced apricots
4 egg whites
¾ cup skim milk
1 tablespoon vegetable oil
½ cup honey

• • •

Topping:
1 cup all-purpose flour
¼ cup cholesterol-free margarine
3 tablespoons whole rolled oats
½ teaspoon cinnamon
¼ cup sugar

Combine the oat bran, Miller's bran, whole wheat flour, baking powder, ½ teaspoon cinnamon, apricots, egg whites, skim milk, oil, and honey. Pour into greased muffin tins. Combine the all-purpose flour, margarine, oats, ½ teaspoon of cinnamon, and sugar, and sprinkle over the muffin batter. Bake at 350° for 15 to 20 minutes. Makes 12 muffins.

Per serving: 121 calories, 22% of calories from fat, 2.02 gm fiber, 0.13 mg cholesterol, 78.8 mg sodium, 3.17 gm fat, 0.44 gm saturated fat, 1.06 gm polyunsaturated fat, 0.94 gm monounsaturated fat.

Carrot Muffins

1 cup whole wheat flour
¾ cup oat bran
2 teaspoons baking powder
½ teaspoon cinnamon
½ teaspoon grated orange peel

Combine the flour, oat bran, baking powder, and spices in a medium bowl. Whisk the juice, molasses, oil, and egg whites together in a large bowl. Stir in the dry ingredients. Add the carrots, raisins, and walnuts, if desired. Divide the batter

¼ teaspoon allspice

⅔ cup unsweetened orange
   juice
¼ cup molasses
¼ cup safflower oil
4 egg whites

½ cup finely grated carrot
⅓ cup raisins (optional)
⅓ cup walnuts (optional)

among greased muffin cups, filling each about ⅔ full. Bake at 375° for about 20 minutes, until the tops are brown.
   Makes 12 muffins.

Per serving: 148 calories, 37% of calories from fat, 2.88 gm fiber, 0.00 mg cholesterol, 76.6 mg sodium, 6.41 gm fat, 0.55 gm saturated fat, 4.21 gm polyunsaturated fat, 0.83 gm monounsaturated fat.

Cranberry-Oat Bran Muffins

½ cup chopped raw
   cranberries
2 tablespoons honey
2 tablespoons vegetable oil
2 egg whites
¾ cup unsweetened orange
   juice
¾ cup oat bran
1 cup whole wheat flour
1 tablespoon baking powder
1 tablespoon grated orange
   rind

Place the cranberries, honey, oil, egg whites and orange juice in a blender or food processor and pulsate until well blended. Combine all of the dry ingredients in a bowl. Make a well in the center of the dry ingredients and add the liquids. Stir with a wooden spoon until well moistened and mixed well. Fill greased muffin tins ⅔ full. Bake at 350° for 20 minutes or until a toothpick inserted in the center comes out clean.
   Makes 12 muffins.

Per serving: 95 calories, 25% of calories from fat, 2.26 gm fiber, 0.00 mg cholesterol, 93.7 mg sodium, 2.88 gm fat, 0.37 gm saturated fat, 0.86 gm polyunsaturated fat, 0.98 gm monounsaturated fat.

Cranberry-Orange Muffins

½ cup fresh or frozen cranberries
2 egg whites
½ cup orange juice
1 tablespoon vegetable oil
1 teaspoon grated orange
  rind
1 cup all-purpose flour
½ cup oat bran
2 teaspoons baking powder
½ teaspoon baking soda
½ cup brown sugar
1 teaspoon vanilla extract
¼ cup chopped walnuts

Mix all of the ingredients together and pour into greased muffin tins. Bake at 350° for 20 minutes. Makes 12 muffins.

Per serving: 120 calories, 22% of calories from fat, 0.97 gm fiber, 0.00 mg cholesterol, 102 mg sodium, 3.06 gm fat, 0.32 gm saturated fat, 1.41 gm polyunsaturated fat, 0.85 gm monounsaturated fat.

Dried Fruit Muffins

2 cups oat bran
½ cup whole wheat pastry
  flour
1 tablespoon baking soda
¼ teaspoon cinnamon
1 cup orange juice
⅓ cup vegetable oil
2 egg whites
1 tablespoon honey
½ cup chopped walnuts
½ cup mixed dried fruits,
  such as peaches, apri-
  cots, raisins, apples

Combine all of the ingredients, stirring gently until well blended. Spoon into greased muffin tins ⅔ full. Bake at 350° for 20 minutes. Makes 12 muffins.

Per serving: 182 calories, 46% of calories from fat, 3.37 gm fiber, 0.00 mg cholesterol, 215 mg sodium, 10.2 gm fat, 1.18 gm saturated fat, 4.23 gm polyunsaturated fat, 3.30 gm monounsaturated fat.

Oat Bran Muffins

¾ cup whole wheat flour
¾ cup oat bran
2 tablespoons baking
  powder
½ teaspoon cinnamon

    •   •   •

3 tablespoons vegetable oil
  (or safflower oil)
3 tablespoons maple syrup
  or honey
¾ cup orange juice

Mix the dry ingredients in a small bowl. Combine the remaining ingredients in a large bowl. Add the dry ingredients and mix until blended. Fill 6 to 8 oiled muffin tins ¾ full. Bake at 375° for 15 minutes.

Makes 6 to 8 muffins.

Per serving: 198 calories, 34% of calories from fat, 3.79 gm fiber, 0.00 mg cholesterol, 340 mg sodium, 7.92 gm fat, 1.05 gm saturated fat, 2.58 gm polyunsaturated fat, 2.94 gm monounsaturated fat.

Oat Bran-Banana Muffins

1 cup whole wheat flour
1 cup all-purpose flour
¾ cup oat bran
2 teaspoons baking powder
¾ teaspoon baking soda
1 teaspoon cinnamon
⅛ teaspoon nutmeg
4 egg whites
2 tablespoons brown sugar
¼ cup vegetable oil
½ cup orange juice
½ cup skim milk
2 bananas, mashed
½ cup toasted sunflower
  seeds (optional)

Combine all of the ingredients, mixing until just blended. Pour into greased muffin tins. Bake at 350° for 20 minutes.

Makes 18 muffins.

Per serving: 136 calories, 35% of calories from fat, 1.95 gm fiber, 0.11 mg cholesterol, 87.5 mg sodium, 5.53 gm fat, 0.72 gm saturated fat, 2.46 gm polyunsaturated fat, 1.69 gm monounsaturated fat.

Pumpkin-Apple Muffins

Batter:
1 cup all-purpose flour
½ cup oat bran
1 teaspoon sugar
2 teaspoons baking powder
½ teaspoon cinnamon
2 tablespoons vegetable oil
½ cup canned pumpkin
2 egg whites
¾ cup orange juice
½ cup diced apple

• • •

Topping:
1 cup wheat germ
¼ cup oat bran
¼ cup all-purpose flour
4 tablespoons cholesterol-
  free margarine

Combine all of the batter ingredients until well-blended. Spoon into greased or paper-lined muffin tins. Combine the topping ingredients and sprinkle over the muffin batter. Bake at 350° for 15 to 20 minutes.

Makes 12 muffins.

Per serving: 176 calories, 38% of calories from fat, 2.20 gm fiber, 0.00 mg cholesterol, 117 mg sodium, 7.74 gm fat, 1.20 gm saturated fat, 3.12 gm polyunsaturated fat, 2.48 gm monounsaturated fat.

Spiced Muffins

4 egg whites
¼ cup vegetable oil
¾ cup unsweetened orange
  juice
⅓ cup sorghum
1 teaspoon vanilla extract
2 cups 100% bran cereal
½ cup raisins

•   •   •

¾ cup whole wheat flour
½ cup oat bran
¼ cup wheat germ
2 teaspoons baking powder
1 teaspoon cinnamon
½ teaspoon nutmeg
Dash ground cloves

Combine the eggs, oil, orange juice, sorghum, and vanilla in a large bowl. Add the bran cereal and raisins. Mix the dry ingredients together in a separate bowl. Stir the dry ingredients into the wet ingredients. Fill greased muffin tins ⅔ full and bake at 375° for 20 minutes or until brown and a toothpick inserted in the center comes out clean.

Makes 12 muffins.

Per serving: 175 calories, 27% of calories from fat, 5.83 gm fiber, 0.00 mg cholesterol, 152 mg sodium, 5.93 gm fat, 0.84 gm saturated fat, 2.19 gm polyunsaturated fat, 2.09 gm monounsaturated fat.

Sunny Bran Muffins

1 cup 3-minute Quick Oats
1½ cups whole wheat flour
1 teaspoon baking powder
½ teaspoon baking soda
1 teaspoon cinnamon
¾ cup oat bran

1½ cups orange juice
4 egg whites
⅔ cup vegetable oil
1 tablespoon grated orange
  peel

½ cup orange marmalade
  (with no sugar added)

Stir together the dry ingredients in a large mixing bowl. Set aside. Combine the orange juice, egg whites, vegetable oil, and orange peel, and mix until well-blended. Add the liquid mixture to the dry ingredients all at once, stirring just until moistened. Gently fold in the orange marmalade, blending well. Fill greased muffin tins ⅔ full. Bake at 375° for 20 minutes or until done.
  Makes 12 muffins.

Per serving: 227 calories, 50% of calories from fat, 2.97 gm fiber, 0.00 mg cholesterol, 79.8 mg sodium, 13.2 gm fat, 1.81 gm saturated fat, 4.52 gm polyunsaturated fat, 5.17 gm monounsaturated fat.

Apple-Raisin Biscuits

⅔ cup crushed oat bran
  flakes
⅔ cup oat bran
2 cups whole pastry flour
2 teaspoons baking powder

1 teaspoon vegetable oil
2 egg whites
¼ cup honey
½ cup plain lowfat yogurt
1 cup raisins
1 cup chopped apple

Combine all the dry ingredients in a mixing bowl. Make a well in the center and add the oil, egg whites, honey, and yogurt. Mix all of the ingredients well. Add the raisins and apple and mix by hand. Roll out on a floured surface until ⅔ inch thick and cut biscuits. Bake at 350° for 20 minutes or until golden brown.
  Makes 18 biscuits.

Per serving: 115 calories, 8% of calories from fat, 3.45 gm fiber, 0.39 mg cholesterol, 49.1 mg sodium, 1.08 gm fat, 0.16 gm saturated fat, 0.12 gm polyunsaturated fat, 0.14 gm monounsaturated fat.

Whole Wheat Yogurt Biscuits

1½ cups whole wheat flour
2 teaspoons baking powder
⅓ teaspoon salt substitute
½ cup oat bran
3 tablespoons vegetable oil
¼ cup skim milk
¼ cup plain lowfat yogurt

Sift together the flour, baking soda, and salt substitute. Add the oat bran to the sifted ingredients. Mix in the oil and work by hand until of the consistency of coarse meal. Add the milk and yogurt and work into a dough. Place on a lightly floured board and roll to a ½-inch thickness. Cut with a biscuit cutter. Place the biscuits on a lightly greased cookie sheet. Bake at 400° for 10 minutes or until golden brown.

Makes 20 biscuits.

Per serving: 58.6 calories, 35% of calories from fat, 1.47 gm fiber, 0.23 mg cholesterol, 37.8 mg sodium, 24.0 gm fat, 0.36 gm saturated fat, 0.77 gm polyunsaturated fat, 0.89 gm monounsaturated fat.

Yogurt Drop Biscuits

1 tablespoon baking powder
¾ teaspoon salt substitute
2 cups sifted all-purpose
   flour
⅓ cup oat bran
¼ cup plain lowfat yogurt
1 cup skim milk

Combine the dry ingredients together and stir in the yogurt and skim milk. Drop the batter into well-greased muffin tins, filling them one-third full. Bake at 425° for about 10 minutes. The batter can be made ahead of time and refrigerated.

Makes 16 biscuits.

Per serving: 71.1 calories, 4% of calories from fat, 0.70 gm fiber, 0.47 mg cholesterol, 74.4 mg sodium, 0.33 gm fat, 0.08 gm saturated fat, 0.00 gm polyunsaturated fat, 0.02 gm monounsaturated fat.

Apple Dressing

2 tablespoons cholesterol-
   free margarine
¼ cup chopped onion
½ cup chopped celery
8 slices day-old Oat Bran
   Bread (see recipe on
   p. 55)
1 cup diced peeled apples
1 teaspoon sage
½ teaspoon salt substitute
¼ teaspoon pepper
½ cup cubed chicken
½ to ¾ cup chicken broth
3 egg whites

Melt the margarine in a skillet and sauté the onion and celery until tender. Crumble the bread into a large bowl and add the onions and celery. Add the apples, seasonings, and cubed chicken. Moisten with the broth as desired. Stir in the egg whites. Use to stuff poultry or bake at 350° for 30 to 40 minutes.
   Serves 4.

Per serving: 44 calories, 39% of calories from fat, 8.55 gm fiber, 48.8 mg cholesterol, 329 mg sodium, 19.9 gm fat, 3.07 gm saturated fat, 8.51 gm polyunsaturated fat, 5.87 gm monounsaturated fat.

Poultry Dressing

6 egg whites
1 medium onion, chopped
3½ to 4 cups low-sodium
   chicken broth
⅛ teaspoon pepper
½ teaspoon sage
½ teaspoon thyme
2 cups diced chicken breast
   meat
½ cup shredded carrots
3 stalks celery, finely
   chopped

1 loaf Oat Bran Bread (see
   recipe on p. 55)

Combine all of the ingredients except the bread. In a large bowl, tear the bread into small bite sized pieces. Pour the liquid ingredients over the bread and stir to moisten. Cover and bake at 350° for 1 hour.
   Serves 8.

Per serving: 406 calories, 31% of calories from fat, 8.37 gm fiber, 58.4 mg cholesterol, 189 mg sodium, 14.5 gm fat, 2.07 gm saturated fat, 5.78 gm polyunsaturated fat, 3.73 gm monounsaturated fat.

Apple Stuffing

¼ cup cholesterol-free margarine
¼ cup diced onion
¾ cup oat bran
½ cup grated and peeled apple
¼ cup chopped celery
¼ cup chopped parsley
¼ teaspoon poultry seasoning
⅛ teaspoon ground black pepper
1 cup Oat Bran Bread crumbs, dried (see recipe on p. 55)
1 cup low-sodium chicken broth

• • •

1 firm apple, unpeeled, cored and thickly sliced
¼ cup water

Melt the margarine in a medium saucepan over medium heat. Sauté the onion in the margarine about 5 minutes. Stir in the oat bran, grated apple, celery, parsley, poultry seasoning, and pepper. Toss with the oat bran bread crumbs. Add the chicken broth to moisten, and place in a baking dish.

Simmer the apple slices in water over low heat for 2 to 4 minutes. Place on top of the dressing. Cover and bake at 375° for 35 to 40 minutes. Serve with baked turkey breast.

Serves 4.

Per serving: 294 calories, 42% of calories from fat, 3.86 gm fiber, 0.00 mg cholesterol, 358 mg sodium, 14.5 gm fat, 2.24 gm saturated fat, 4.98 gm polyunsaturated fat, 4.06 gm monounsaturated fat.

Southern Corn Bread Stuffing

3 cups crumbled corn bread
1 cup Oat Bran Bread
   crumbs (see recipe on
   p. 55)
2 cups chicken broth
3 stalks celery, finely
   chopped
1 large onion, finely
   chopped
2 egg whites
Pepper
½ teaspoon sage
½ teaspoon paprika
2 tablespoons cholesterol-
   free margarine

Combine all of the ingredients except the margarine. Turn into a greased baking dish and dot the top with margarine. Cover and bake at 350° for 30 minutes. Remove the cover and cook for another 15 minutes.

   Serves 4.

Per serving: 342 calories, 40% of calories from fat, 5.00 gm fiber, 13.7 mg cholesterol, 311 mg sodium, 15.5 gm fat, 1.74 gm saturated fat, 4.79 gm polyunsaturated fat, 3.41 gm monounsaturated fat.

Applesauce Pancakes

4 egg whites
½ cup unsweetened orange
  juice
2 tablespoons cholesterol-
  free margarine, melted
1 cup unsweetened ap-
  plesauce
¾ cup oat bran
1 teaspoon cinnamon
¾ cup whole wheat flour
2 tablespoons granulated
  sugar
1 tablespoon baking powder

Beat together the egg whites, orange juice, melted margarine, and applesauce. Stir in the oat bran and cinnamon. Let the mixture stand for 5 minutes. Combine the flour, sugar, and baking powder in a separate bowl. Fold into the bran mixture, stirring just until moistened. Spoon approximately ¼ cup of batter at a time onto a hot, lightly buttered griddle. Allow to cook until bubbly on top and browned on the bottom. Turn and brown on the other side. Serve immediately. Serve with margarine and syrup.

Makes 12 pancakes.

Per serving: 87.4 calories, 24% of calories from fat, 2.20 gm fiber, 0.00 mg cholesterol, 128 mg sodium, 2.47 gm fat, 0.36 gm saturated fat, 0.83 gm polyunsaturated fat, 0.68 gm monounsaturated fat.

Buckwheat Yogurt Pancakes

1½ cups buckwheat flour
⅓ cup oat bran
¾ teaspoon salt substitute
1 teaspoon baking soda
1½ cups lowfat buttermilk
½ cup plain lowfat yogurt
1 egg, beaten, or egg substitute
1 teaspoon maple flavoring
1 tablespoon vegetable oil

Combine the flour, oat bran, salt substitute, and baking soda. Add the buttermilk, yogurt, egg, maple flavoring, and oil. Pour on a hot, lightly oiled griddle and cook until brown, turning once. Serve hot.

Makes 16 pancakes.

Per serving: 63.7 calories, 24% of calories from fat, 0.26 gm fiber, 18.4 mg cholesterol, 84.9 mg sodium, 1.73 gm fat, 0.44 gm saturated fat, 0.38 gm polyunsaturated fat, 0.59 gm monounsaturated fat.

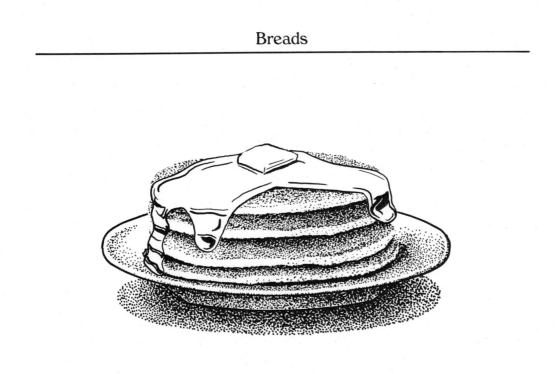

Cornmeal Griddle Cakes

1 cup cornmeal
½ cup all-purpose flour
⅓ cup oat bran
1 teaspoon salt substitute
1⅓ tablespoons baking
   powder
1 egg, beaten or egg sub-
   stitute
1½ cups lowfat buttermilk
½ cup plain lowfat yogurt
¼ cup vegetable oil

Mix the dry ingredients in a small bowl. Combine the egg and buttermilk in a large bowl. Blend in the yogurt. Add the dry ingredients and stir to make a smooth batter. Stir in the oil. Bake on a hot oiled griddle, turning when the underside is browned and the batter is bubbly.

Makes 18 pancakes.

Per serving: 89.9 calories, 38% of calories from fat, 0.33 gm fiber, 16.4 mg cholesterol, 105 mg sodium, 3.87 gm fat, 0.73 gm saturated fat, 1.19 gm polyunsaturated fat, 1.51 gm monounsaturated fat.

Corn Cakes

1½ cups lowfat buttermilk
1 tablespoon safflower oil
1 teaspoon baking soda
1 egg white
1 teaspoon salt substitute
⅔ cup corn meal
⅓ cup oat bran
¼ cup all-purpose flour

Combine all of the ingredients and mix well. Drop by heaping tablespoons onto a hot griddle. Cook until golden on each side.
Serves 4.

Per serving: 205 calories, 22% of calories from fat, 1.24 gm fiber, 3.38 mg cholesterol, 316 mg sodium, 5.11 gm fat, 1.05 gm saturated fat, 1.31 gm polyunsaturated fat, 1.70 gm monounsaturated fat.

Pancakes

1½ cups quick or old-fashioned rolled oats
3 tablespoons oat bran
1 tablespoon baking powder
1 tablespoon whole wheat flour
1½ cups skim milk
3 egg whites
1 tablespoon vegetable oil

Process the oats, oat bran, baking powder, and whole wheat flour together in a blender. Mix the liquid ingredients until well combined. Let stand for 5 minutes. Bake on a hot griddle, turning with a spatula when the edges get firm.
Makes 10 pancakes.

Per serving: 89 calories, 24% of calories from fat, 0.34 gm fiber, 0.60 mg cholesterol, 136 mg sodium, 2.56 gm fat, 0.24 gm saturated fat, 0.52 gm polyunsaturated fat, 0.60 gm monounsaturated fat.

Oat Bran Croutons

1 loaf Oat Bran Bread (see
  recipe on p. 55)
¼ cup cholesterol-free margarine, melted
1 tablespoon dried parsley
1 teaspoon ground sage
1 teaspoon onion powder
1 teaspoon garlic powder

Cut the loaf of bread first into slices and then into cubes in a large bowl. Set aside. Combine in a separate bowl the margarine, parsley, sage, onion powder, and garlic powder. Drizzle the margarine mixture over the bread cubes, lightly stirring to combine all of the ingredients. Place the bread cubes in a single layer on a cookie sheet and bake at 300° for 15 minutes. Remove from the oven and allow to cool.

Serves 8.

Per serving: 358 calories, 43% of calories from fat, 7.09 gm fiber, 34.3 mg cholesterol, 164 mg sodium, 18.2 gm fat, 2.73 gm saturated fat, 7.95 gm polyunsaturated fat, 5.38 gm monounsaturated fat.

Scottish Oat Cakes

4 cups rolled oats
½ cup all-purpose flour
¼ cup oat bran
1½ teaspoons baking
  powder
½ cup cholesterol-free margarine
2 to 3 tablespoons skim
  milk

Process the oats in a food processor until fine. Combine with the remaining ingredients to form a stiff dough. Let the dough rest for 30 minutes. Roll out to ¼-inch thickness on a floured surface. Cut into circles. Bake at 350° for 8 to 10 minutes or until golden brown.

Makes 12 cakes.

Per serving: 194 calories, 43% of calories from fat, 0.42 gm fiber, 0.04 mg cholesterol, 146 mg sodium, 9.80 gm fat, 1.32 gm saturated fat, 3.28 gm polyunsaturated fat, 2.70 gm monounsaturated fat.

Cinnamon French Toast

8 egg whites
8 tablespoons skim milk
1 teaspoon vanilla extract
½ teaspoon cinnamon

• • •

5 tablespoons cholesterol-
free margarine

• • •

8 slices day old Oat Bran
Bread slices (see recipe
on p. 55)

Lightly beat the egg whites, skim milk, vanilla, and cinnamon together. Heat a griddle and lightly grease with margarine. Coat both sides of each bread slice with the egg white mixture. Cook until brown and crisp.
Serves 4.

Per serving: 498 calories, 48% of calories from fat, 7.56 gm fiber, 37.1 mg cholesterol, 400 mg sodium, 27.7 gm fat, 4.35 gm saturated fat, 12.0 gm polyunsaturated fat, 8.65 gm monounsaturated fat.

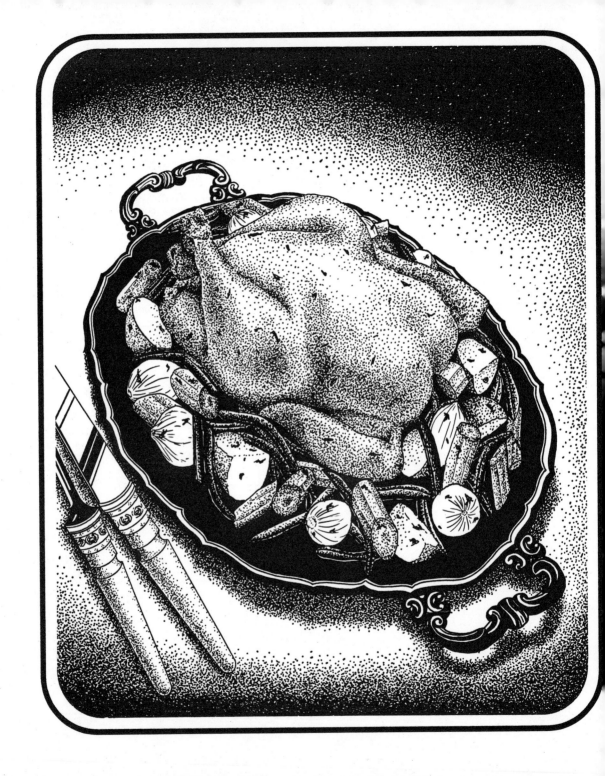

ENTREES

Apple Pot Roast

3 to 4 pounds beef blade
    pot roast
¼ cup all-purpose flour
3 tablespoons oat bran
¼ teaspoon pepper
Vegetable oil
2 medium onions, sliced
½ cup beef broth or apple
    juice
1 acorn squash or large
    piece of winter squash
    (about 1 pound)
2 tart apples, cored and
    quartered

Trim the surface fat from the roast. Combine the flour, oat bran, and pepper, and coat the meat. Brown the meat in oil, turning to brown on all sides. Pour off the excess drippings. Add the onions and cook until they are tender but not browned. Add the water or broth. Cover and simmer for 2 hours. Peel the squash and scrape off any seeds and stringy pulp. Slice or cube the squash and add it to the pot roast along with the apples. Cover and simmer 30 minutes longer or until the meat and vegetables are tender.
    Serves 8.

Per serving: 578 calories, 42% of calories from fat, 4.33 gm fiber 180 mg cholesterol, 126 mg sodium, 26.7 gm fat, 10.7 gm saturated fat, 1.08 gm polyunsaturated fat, 11.7 gm monounsaturated fat.

Hot and Spicy Meat Loaf

Meat Loaf:
2 pounds lean ground beef
1 pound white turkey breast
    meat, ground
1 medium onion, chopped
2 ribs celery, finely chopped
1 teaspoon dried rosemary
1 teaspoon tarragon
1 teaspoon thyme
2 teaspoons minced fresh
    parsley
¼ teaspoon black pepper
10 drops hot red pepper
    sauce
4 egg whites
1 cup tomato sauce
1 tablespoon minced garlic
1½ cups oat bran
1 cup chopped red and
    green peppers
1 cup skim milk

．　　．　　．

Sauce:
½ cup tomato sauce
1 tablespoon Wor-
    cestershire sauce
¼ cup finely chopped mild
    red peppers

Combine in a large bowl all of the meat loaf ingredients. Form the mixture into a loaf and place in a greased loaf pan. Bake covered at 350° for 1 hour.

Combine the tomato sauce, Worcestershire sauce, and red peppers in a small mixing bowl. When the meat loaf has cooked for 1 hour, uncover and pour the sauce over the meat. Return to the oven and cook an additional 15 minutes.

Serves 8.

Per serving: 485 calories, 38% of calories from fat, 4.10 gm fiber, 143 mg cholesterol, 456 mg sodium, 20.6 gm fat, 7.52 gm saturated fat, 1.04 gm polyunsaturated fat, 8.25 gm monounsaturated fat.

Mini Meat Loaves

2 egg whites
1 pound lean ground beef
1 pound lean ground white
  turkey meat
¾ cup oat bran
1 8-ounce can tomato sauce
2 tablespoons minced onion
1 teaspoon chili powder
1 teaspoon Italian seasoning mix
1 cup water
1 teaspoon minced garlic

• • •

½ cup tomato sauce
½ cup shredded reduced
  calorie Mozzarella cheese

Combine all of the ingredients except the tomato sauce and cheese. Form into 8 small loaves. Place in greased individual loaf pans. Cover and bake at 350° for 35 minutes. Uncover and spread the tomato sauce over each loaf. Top with Mozzarella cheese. Return to the oven and bake an additional 10 minutes. Remove and serve.
  Serves 8.

Per serving: 285 calories, 36% of calories from fat, 1.28 gm fiber, 98.7 mg cholesterol, 393 mg sodium, 11.5 gm fat, 4.51 gm saturated fat, 0.52 gm polyunsaturated fat, 4.46 gm monounsaturated fat.

Christmas Night Miniature Meatballs

2 tablespoons soy sauce
¼ cup water
3 tablespoons oat bran
½ clove garlic, minced
½ teaspoon nutmeg
1 pound lean ground chuck

Combine the soy sauce, water, oat bran, garlic, and nutmeg in a large bowl. Stir to blend. Add the ground chuck and mix lightly, but thoroughly. Form into meatballs 1 inch in diameter. Arrange in a lightly oiled baking dish. Bake uncovered for 15 minutes. Place on a heated tray or in a chafing dish. Serve with toothpicks.

Makes approximately 32 meatballs.

Per serving: 38.6 calories, 56% of calories from fat, 0.07 gm fiber, 11.8 mg cholesterol, 74.2 mg sodium, 2.36 gm fat, 0.91 gm saturated fat, 0.09 gm polyunsaturated fat, 1.01 gm monounsaturated fat.

Swedish Meatballs

1 pound lean ground beef
½ cup oat bran
1 onion, diced
Egg substitute equivalent to
   1 egg
1 teaspoon Worcestershire
   sauce
1 tablespoon parsley flakes
1 teaspoon pepper
1 10¾-ounce can cream of
   celery soup
1 soup can skim milk

Combine the ground beef, oat bran, onion, egg substitute, Worcestershire sauce and seasonings in a mixing bowl. Add ¼ cup of soup to the mixture and form into meatballs. Bake at 350° on a shallow baking sheet. Combine the remaining soup and skim milk in a medium saucepan to make a sauce. Add the meatballs and heat for about 15 minutes.

Serves 8.

Per serving: 228 calories, 45% of calories from fat, 1.87 gm fiber, 53.0 mg cholesterol, 238 mg sodium, 11.4 gm fat, 4.32 gm saturated fat, 0.82 gm polyunsaturated fat, 4.48 gm monounsaturated fat.

Beef, Macaroni, and Tomato Casserole

⅔ cup uncooked macaroni
3 cups water

• • •

1 pound lean ground beef
¼ cup finely chopped
  onion
1 tablespoon finely chopped
  celery
¼ cup finely chopped green
  pepper
1 tablespoon Wor-
  cestershire sauce
1 tablespoon soy sauce

• • •

1 cup canned pureed
  tomatoes
1 cup salt-free tomato juice
1 cup cooked kidney beans
⅛ teaspoon pepper
¼ teaspoon basil leaves
1 teaspoon parsley flakes

Cook the macaroni in water until tender. Drain and rinse with cold water. Set aside. Combine the ground beef, onion, celery, green pepper, Worcestershire and soy sauces. Cook until the beef is browned and the vegetables are tender. Combine the canned tomatoes, tomato juice, kidney beans, pepper, basil leaves, and parsley flakes in a large pot. Add the ground beef mixture and bring to a boil. Reduce to a simmer and stir in the macaroni. Simmer until all is warmed throughout.

Serves 4.

Per serving: 543 calories, 33% of calories from fat, 5.77 gm fiber, 94.7 mg cholesterol, 688 mg sodium, 20.0 gm fat, 7.32 gm saturated fat, 0.85 gm polyunsaturated fat, 8.15 gm monounsaturated fat.

Chicken-Filled Oat Bran Popovers

Popovers:
2 egg whites
1 cup skim milk
½ cup all-purpose flour
½ cup oat bran
2 tablespoons corn oil margarine

· · ·

Filling:
1 cup finely chopped cooked chicken
½ cup finely chopped celery
½ cup reduced-calorie mayonnaise
2 tablespoons Italian dressing
1 teaspoon prepared mustard
2 green onions finely chopped
Mrs. Dash seasoning
Paprika to taste

Beat the egg whites, milk, flour, oat bran and margarine. Pour into well-greased deep muffin or popover pans, filling ⅔ full. Bake at 375° for 20 to 25 minutes. Do not open the oven while cooking or these will collapse.

Combine the chicken, celery, mayonnaise, dressing, mustard, and onion. Stir well. Sprinkle with Mrs. Dash and paprika to taste. Open the popovers and stuff the inside.

Serves 6.

Per serving: 241 calories, 49% of calories from fat, 1.53 gm fiber, 31.4 mg cholesterol, 168 mg sodium, 13.2 gm fat, 1.34 gm saturated fat, 3.23 gm polyunsaturated fat, 2.29 gm monounsaturated fat.

Baked Chicken and Rice

4 chicken breasts, skinned
and boned
¼ cup cholesterol-free margarine

1 medium onion, chopped

1 10¾-ounce can cream of
chicken soup, undiluted
⅔ cup dry white wine
1 tablespoon chopped par-
sley
1 teaspoon paprika
Pepper to taste
1 tablespoon soy sauce
1 tablespoon lemon juice

Hot cooked wild brown rice
Lemon slices and parsley
for garnish

Lightly brown the chicken breasts in margarine in a covered skillet. Remove the chicken from the skillet and place in a baking dish. Add the onions to the margarine remaining in the skillet and cook until tender but not brown. Add the soup, wine, seasonings, soy sauce, and lemon juice. Blend thoroughly and pour over the chicken. Bake at 350° for about 45 minutes. Remove from the oven. Place the chicken on a bed of brown rice, and garnish with lemon slices and parsley.
    Serves 4.

Per serving: 608 calories, 31% of calories from fat, 5.24 gm fiber, 149 mg cholesterol, 849 mg sodium, 20.8 gm fat, 4.40 gm saturated fat, 6.81 gm polyunsaturated fat, 7.25 gm monounsaturated fat.

Poultry and Rice Pilaf

2 cups chicken broth
½ cup long grain rice
½ teaspoon cinnamon
¼ teaspoon black pepper
3 tablespoons pine nuts
8 chicken breasts, split and
　boned, or 1 turkey breast
2 tablespoons cholesterol-
　free margarine, melted
½ clove garlic, mashed
Juice of ½ lemon
1 teaspoon oregano
Parsley

Place the broth in a large pot and add the rice, cinnamon, pepper, and pine nuts. Cook for 5 minutes over low heat, stirring often. Reduce the heat and simmer for 20 minutes or until the rice is done. Place the boned chicken or turkey in a foil-lined pan. Combine the melted margarine, garlic, lemon juice, and oregano and brush on the chicken. Seal the foil. Bake at 350° for 30 minutes. Uncover for the last 10 minutes. Serve the hot rice mixture on a large platter topped with the chicken pieces. Garnish with parsley.
Serves 8.

Per serving: 369 calories, 27% of calories from fat, 0.35 gm fiber, 146 mg cholesterol, 165 mg sodium, 10.5 gm fat, 2.53 gm saturated fat, 2.80 gm polyunsaturated fat, 4.02 gm monounsaturated fat.

Breaded Chicken Breast Strips

1 cup oat bran
¼ cup all-purpose flour
½ teaspoon black pepper
½ teaspoon paprika
2 egg whites
6 chicken breast fillets,
　skinned and boned
¼ cup vegetable oil

Combine the oat bran, flour, pepper, and paprika in a shallow bowl. Place the egg whites in a second bowl. Dip the chicken breast fillets in the egg whites and then dredge with the oat bran mixture. Heat the oil in a skillet over medium high heat. Stir-fry the chicken pieces until tender and crisp.
Serves 6.

Per serving: 434 calories, 34% of calories from fat, 2.19 gm fiber, 146 mg cholesterol, 143 mg sodium, 16 gm fat, 3.08 gm saturated fat, 4.73 gm polyunsaturated fat, 6.05 gm monounsaturated fat.

Cheese and Sesame Chicken

2 pounds boneless and
  skinless chicken breast
  fillets
1 cup milk
1 cup crushed cheese
  crackers
¼ cup oat bran
2 tablespoons sesame
  seeds
Paprika and garlic powder
  to taste
1 tablespoon cholesterol-
  free margarine, melted

Soak the chicken breasts in milk. Combine the cracker crumbs and oat bran, and roll the chicken in the mixture. Place in a baking dish. Sprinkle with sesame seeds, paprika, and garlic powder to taste. Drizzle all of the chicken pieces with margarine. Cover and bake at 350° for 30 to 45 minutes, until tender and the juices run clear. Uncover for the last 5 to 10 minutes to give a crusty topping.

Serves 8.

Per serving: 155 calories, 39% of calories from fat, 0.92 gm fiber, 37.0 mg cholesterol, 152 mg sodium, 6.65 gm fat, 1.51 gm saturated fat, 1.44 gm polyunsaturated fat, 1.48 gm monounsaturated fat.

Gingered Lime Chicken

½ teaspoon pepper
2 large cloves garlic, minced
1 tablespoon minced fresh
  ginger
½ cup all-purpose flour
½ cup oat bran
2 split chicken breasts
¼ cup safflower oil
Juice of 1 whole lime
Parsley
Lime wedges

Combine the spices, flour, and oat bran. Coat the chicken well in the flour and spice mixture. Cook the chicken pieces in hot oil until lightly brown on both sides. Remove and place in a baking dish. Squeeze the juice from 1 lime over both pieces. Cover and bake at 350° for 30 minutes. Remove the cover and bake an additional 10 minutes. Place on a serving dish and garnish with parsley and lime wedges.

Serves 2.

Per serving: 761 calories, 42% of calories from fat, 5.99 gm fiber, 146 mg cholesterol, 127 mg sodium, 36.2 gm fat, 5.77 gm saturated fat, 11.6 gm polyunsaturated fat, 13.9 gm monounsaturated fat.

Herbed Chicken or Turkey

2 whole chickens or 1 large
   turkey
7 cloves garlic
2 bay leaves
   •   •

6 tablespoons cholesterol-
   free margarine
1 teaspoon pepper
½ teaspoon thyme leaves
½ teaspoon rubbed sage
½ teaspoon oregano
½ teaspoon marjoram
½ teaspoon dry basil
  •   •   •

½ cup oat bran, toasted

Rinse and dry the chickens or turkey. Rub the skin with a clove of the garlic. Stuff the cavity with the bay leaves and garlic cloves. Melt the margarine in a saucepan and add the remaining ingredients. Spread the margarine-herb mixture over each chicken or turkey. Sprinkle with oat bran. Cover and bake at 350° for 1½ hours or until tender.

Serves 16.

Per serving: 404 calories, 31% of calories from fat, 0.41 gm fiber, 137 mg cholesterol, 128 mg sodium, 22.7 gm fat, 6 gm saturated fat, 5.35 gm polyunsaturated fat, 9.45 gm monounsaturated fat.

Parmesan Chicken

1¼ cups oat bran
⅓ cup Parmesan cheese
½ teaspoon paprika
¼ teaspoon black pepper
  •   •   •

⅓ cup skim milk
4 whole chicken breasts,
   split in half

Combine the oat bran, Parmesan, paprika, and pepper in a shallow bowl. Put the milk into a separate bowl. Soak the chicken in the milk for 15 minutes. Dredge the chicken in the oat bran mixture and place in an oiled baking dish. Bake at 350° for 40 to 45 minutes.

Serves 8.

Per serving: 207 calories, 23% of calories from fat, 1.94 gm fiber, 76.4 mg cholesterol, 145 mg sodium, 5.27 gm fat, 1.67 gm saturated fat, 0.69 gm polyunsaturated fat, 1.44 gm monounsaturated fat.

Stir-Fried Chicken

1 cup chicken broth
2 tablespoons soy sauce
2 tablespoons Worcestershire sauce
¼ teaspoon garlic powder
½ cup chopped onion
1 cup diced celery

     •   •   •

2 cups diced cooked
  chicken
1 cup bean sprouts
1 cup bamboo shoots
1 8-ounce can sliced water
  chestnuts
1 6-ounce can sliced mushrooms
1 6-ounce package frozen
  snow peas, thawed

     •   •   •

2 cups hot cooked rice
Rice noodles

Heat the broth until simmering. Add the soy sauce, Worcestershire sauce, garlic powder, onion, and celery. Cook for 5 to 6 minutes. Add the remaining ingredients and cook for 10 minutes. Serve over hot rice and top with rice noodles.
   Serves 4.

Per serving: 356 calories, 10% of calories from fat, 3.98 gm fiber, 72.5 mg cholesterol, 946 mg sodium, 3.82 gm fat, 1.11 gm saturated fat, 0.88 gm polyunsaturated fat, 1.24 gm monounsaturated fat.

Orange-Spiced Chicken Drumsticks

1 tablespoon whole wheat
flour

.   .   .

Egg substitute equivalent to
1 egg
1 tablespoon skim milk

.   .   .

½ cup oat bran
Grated peel of 1 orange
1 teaspoon curry powder

.   .   .

6 chicken drumsticks

Place the flour in a small bowl. Combine the egg substitute and skim milk in a separate bowl. Combine the oat bran, orange peel, and curry powder in a third bowl. Wash the drumsticks and dip each first in the flour, then in the egg and milk mixture, and then coat with the oat bran mixture. Arrange in an ungreased baking dish. Bake at 350° for 30 minutes or until tender and the juices run clear.
Serves 6.

Per serving: 299 calories, 48% of calories from fat, 1.25 gm fiber, 105 mg cholesterol, 117 mg sodium, 15.9 gm fat, 4.23 gm saturated fat, 3.43 gm polyunsaturated fat, 5.96 gm monounsaturated fat.

Baked Chicken Livers

1 pound chicken livers
½ cup milk
¾ cup oat bran
¼ cup whole wheat flour
1 cube chicken bouillon dissolved in ½ cup water
1 medium onion, slivered
Paprika

Soak the chicken livers in milk. Combine the oat bran and flour, and roll the livers in the mixture. Place in a baking dish. Pour the dissolved bouillon over the livers. Top with onion. Sprinkle with paprika, cover, and bake at 350° for 1 hour or until tender.
Serves 4.

Per serving: 307 calories, 22% of calories from fat, 5.27 gm fiber, 716 mg cholesterol, 292 mg sodium, 7.89 gm fat, 2.22 gm saturated fat, 1.13 gm polyunsaturated fat, 1.59 gm monounsaturated fat.

Quick and Easy Pizzas

1 pound ground turkey
  breast meat
3 tablespoons oat bran
¼ teaspoon finely ground
  parsley
½ teaspoon Italian seasoning
  .   .   .

¼ cup chopped onions
⅛ cup chopped green pep-
  per
1 tablespoon cholesterol-
  free margarine
  .   .   .

2 English muffins, split
4 tablespoons tomato sauce
¼ cup shredded lowfat
  Mozzarella cheese
Parmesan cheese

Combine the turkey breast meat, oat bran, parsley, and Italian seasoning. Set aside. Sauté the onions and green peppers in margarine in a sauté pan for 5 minutes, then drain. Place the halved English muffins on a cookie sheet. Layer with tomato sauce, the onion and pepper mixture, turkey mixture, and the cheeses. Toast under a broiler until warmed throughout and the cheese is bubbly.

Serves 4.

Per serving: 296 calories, 21% of calories from fat, 0.65 gm fiber, 101 mg cholesterol, 460 mg sodium, 6.66 gm fat, 2.09 gm saturated fat, 1.52 gm polyunsaturated fat, 1.76 gm monounsaturated fat.

Turkey Loaf

1 pound ground turkey
  breast
1 egg white
⅓ cup oat bran
3 tablespoons catsup
1 tablespoon Wor-
  cestershire sauce
1 tablespoon soy sauce
½ green pepper, minced
1 small onion, minced
1 teaspoon minced garlic
¼ teaspoon celery salt
¼ teaspoon sage
¼ teaspoon pepper
¼ teaspoon marjoram

•   •   •

Onion slices

Mix all of the ingredients well in a large bowl. Form into a loaf and place in an oiled baking pan. Cover and bake at 350° for 1 hour. Uncover and top with onion rings. Bake an additional 15 minutes.
  Serves 4.

Per serving: 219 calories, 6% of calories from fat, 2.14 gm fiber, 94.5 mg cholesterol, 613 mg sodium, 1.40 gm fat, 0.31 gm saturated fat, 0.33 gm polyunsaturated fat, 0.18 gm monounsaturated fat.

Oat Bran Meatballs

1 pound lean ground turkey
½ cup oat bran
1 clove garlic, crushed
2 tablespoons water
2 egg whites
¼ cup diced onion

Combine all of the ingredients. Shape into balls, using 1 tablespoonful of meat for each ball. Place on a baking sheet. Bake at 350° for 15 to 20 minutes or until browned. Serve with stir-fried vegetables.
  Makes 24 meatballs.

Per serving: 33.4 calories, 8% of calories from fat, 0.30 gm fiber, 15.8 mg cholesterol, 14.0 mg sodium, 0.28 gm fat, 0.05 gm saturated fat, 0.04 gm polyunsaturated fat, 0.03 gm monounsaturated fat.

Oat Bran Patties

1 large carrot, peeled
2 tablespoons chopped
  onion
1 1-inch slice green pepper
1 rib celery
1 tablespoon parsley

.   .   .

1 cup rolled oats, cut in food
  processor
3 egg whites
⅓ cup oat bran
1 tablespoon soy sauce
1 tablespoon safflower oil
⅛ teaspoon dried basil
¼ cup tomato juice
1 tablespoon brown mus-
  tard

Combine the vegetables in a food processor and process until finely chopped. Combine the oats, chopped vegetables, egg whites, oat bran, soy sauce, oil, basil, tomato juice, and brown mustard in a large mixing bowl. Shape into 4 patties. If the mixture is too crumbly, add more liquid. Place in an oiled pan. Bake at 350° for 20 minutes. Turn the patties over and bake for another 20 minutes. Drain on a paper towel to remove excess oil and fat.

Serves 4.

Per serving: 160 calories, 30% of calories from fat, 1.95 gm fiber, 0.00 mg cholesterol, 416 mg sodium, 5.74 gm fat, 0.51 gm saturated fat, 1.32 gm polyunsaturated fat, 1.47 gm monounsaturated fat.

Crab Cakes

¼ cup cholesterol-free margarine
2 tablespoons minced onion
½ cup finely chopped celery
2 cups crabmeat
½ teaspoon dry mustard
3 egg whites, beaten
½ cup skim milk
1 cup oat bran
Paprika to taste

Melt the margarine in a sauté pan. Add the onion and celery and sauté until tender. Combine the crab meat, dry mustard, egg whites, milk, oat bran (reserving 2 tablespoons for garnishing the top), celery, and onion. Form into patties and place in a greased baking dish. Sprinkle the tops of the crab cakes with paprika and the reserved oat bran. Bake at 350° for 25 to 30 minutes.
    Serves 6.

Per serving: 176 calories, 47% of calories from fat, 2.21 gm fiber, 45.3 mg cholesterol, 371 mg sodium, 9.68 gm fat, 1.53 gm saturated fat, 4.04 gm polyunsaturated fat, 2.97 gm monounsaturated fat.

Baked Fish

1 pound sole, flounder or perch fillets, fresh or frozen
Juice of 1 lemon
¼ teaspoon salt substitute
Dash fresh ground pepper
2 tablespoons vegetable oil
⅓ cup oat bran

Wash and dry the fish fillets, then cut into serving size pieces, allowing for shrinkage. Rub each fillet with the juice of the lemon. Season and then dip in oil. Drain. Coat each piece with the oat bran. Arrange in a greased baking dish in a single layer. Bake at 350° for 30 minutes or until the fish flakes easily.
    Serves 4.

Per serving: 308 calories, 49% of calories from fat, 0.80 gm fiber, 0.00 mg cholesterol, 269 mg sodium, 16.5 gm fat, 1.00 gm saturated fat, 2.58 gm polyunsaturated fat, 2.93 gm monounsaturated fat.

Breaded Baked Fish

½ cup oat bran
¼ cup stone ground corn-
 meal
2 teaspoons dry mustard
1 teaspoon paprika
 •   •   •

¼ cup skim milk
2 egg whites, beaten
 •   •   •

¼ cup safflower oil
4 fish fillets
¼ cup dry white wine

Combine the oat bran, cornmeal, mustard, and paprika. Combine the milk and egg whites in a separate bowl. Heat the oil in a sauté pan. Dip the fillets in the bran mixture to coat, then the egg mixture, and back into the bran mixture again. Sauté until browned on both sides. Place in a baking dish. Add the wine and bake at 350° for 20 minutes. Garnish with lemon slice and parsley.
 Serves 4.

Per serving: 421 calories, 49% of calories from fat, 1.64 gm fiber, 0.25 mg cholesterol, 271 mg sodium, 22.8 gm fat, 2.02 gm saturated fat, 5.13 gm polyunsaturated fat, 5.87 gm monounsaturated fat.

Seaman's Fish Bake

¼ cup enriched cornmeal
¼ cup oat bran
¼ teaspoon nutmeg
½ teaspoon paprika
¼ teaspoon pepper
 •   •   •

Egg substitute equivalent to
 1 egg
2 tablespoons milk
 •   •   •

1 pound fresh or frozen
 cod, halibut or sole fish
 fillets, thawed
2 tablespoons cholesterol-
 free margarine, melted

Combine the cornmeal, oat bran, nutmeg, paprika, and pepper. Combine the egg substitute and milk. Dip the fish in the milk mixture, and then coat with the cornmeal mixture. Place in a shallow pan and drizzle with melted margarine. Bake at 350° for 15 to 20 minutes or until golden brown.
 Serves 6.

Per serving: 226 calories, 42% of calories from fat, 0.55 gm fiber, 0.04 mg cholesterol, 248 mg sodium, 10.4 gm fat, 0.66 gm saturated fat, 1.64 gm polyunsaturated fat, 1.35 gm monounsaturated fat.

Flounder Parmigiana

1 pound flounder fillets, cut
    into 4 serving pieces
½ cup skim milk
¾ cup oat bran
½ cup Parmesan cheese
⅛ teaspoon paprika
2 tablespoons safflower oil
1 small onion, finely
    chopped

Soak the flounder in skim milk for 15 minutes. Combine the oat bran, Parmesan cheese, and paprika. Dredge the fish with the mixture, coating each side. Place the oil in a baking dish. Layer the onion across the bottom of the dish. Place the coated fish fillets on top and sprinkle with the remaining oat bran mixture. Bake at 350° until the fish flakes with a fork, approximately 20 to 30 minutes. Garnish with a lemon wedge and parsley.

Serves 4.

Per serving: 440 calories, 60% of calories from fat, 3.86 gm fiber, 10.4 mg cholesterol, 519 mg sodium, 21.3 gm fat, 3.46 gm saturated fat, 2.73 gm polyunsaturated fat, 4.07 gm monounsaturated fat.

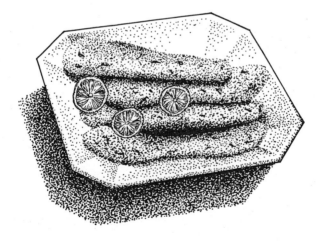

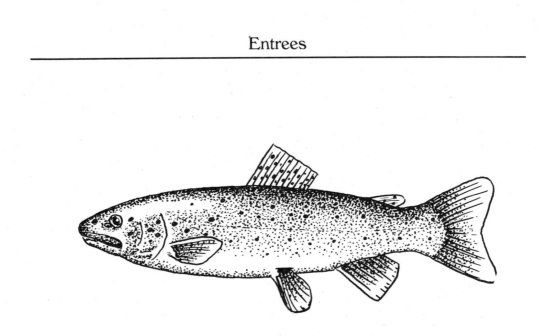

Trout Bake

4 trout fillets, halved
1 cup milk
¾ cup oat bran
4 tablespoons cholesterol-
   free margarine, melted
½ cup roasted almonds

Soak the trout in milk for 1 hour before cooking. Drain. Combine the oat bran and melted margarine in a separate bowl and mix well. Dredge the trout in the oat bran and place in a baking dish. Sprinkle the tops of the fillets with almonds. Bake uncovered at 350° for 30 minutes or until the fish flakes easily.
   Serves 8.

Per serving: 234 calories, 60% of calories from fat, 1.98 gm fiber, 0.50 mg cholesterol, 133 mg sodium, 16.2 gm fat, 1.42 gm saturated fat, 3.35 gm polyunsaturated fat, 4.79 gm monounsaturated fat.

Poached Haddock with Leeks and Mussels

½ cup julienne-cut celery
½ cup julienne-cut carrots
½ cup julienne-cut zucchini

* * *

1 cup water (reserved from cooking vegetables)
1 cup dry white wine
½ cup finely sliced leeks or scallions
4 dozen mussels

* * *

2 pounds haddock or cod

* * *

½ cup skim milk
¼ cup oat bran
¼ teaspoon nutmeg
Pepper and paprika to taste
2 tablespoons chopped fresh parsley
¼ cup cholesterol-free margarine

Cook the vegetables in a large saucepan in water to cover until tender but still firm. Drain, reserving 1 cup of water. Set the vegetables aside. Bring the water, wine, and chopped leeks to a simmer. Scrub and debeard the mussels and add to the leeks. Cover and steam. Continue to steam for 5 minutes after the mussels have opened. Remove about half from their shells and reserve the rest, keeping warm for garnish.

Strain the liquid from the steaming mussels into a large skillet and add the fish. Cover and gently simmer for 8 to 10 minutes, until the fish flakes easily. Transfer to an ovenproof platter and keep warm. Reduce the liquid quickly to ½ cup. Add the skim milk, oat bran, seasonings, and butter in small pieces, whisking constantly. Add the shelled mussels and parsley and heat through. Pour the sauce over the fish, top with the vegetables, and garnish with the remaining mussels.

Serves 8.

Per serving: 427 calories, 37% of calories from fat, 0.82 gm fiber, 0.25 mg cholesterol, 663 mg sodium, 17.2 gm fat, 1.00 gm saturated fat, 2.47 gm polyunsaturated fat, 2.03 gm monounsaturated fat.

Baked Salmon Loaf

Salmon Loaf:

1 16-ounce can red salmon,
  including liquid
½ cup rolled oats
½ cup oat bran
½ cup Oat Bran Bread
  crumbs (see recipe on
  p. 55)
¾ cup skim milk
2 egg whites, lightly beaten
1 small onion, finely
  chopped
1 stalk celery, finely
  chopped
⅛ teaspoon black pepper

Sauce:

1 tablespoon minced onion
1 cup fresh mushrooms
1 teaspoon cholesterol-free
  margarine
1 8-ounce can tomato sauce

Combine the loaf ingredients in a large bowl and mix well. Form into a loaf. Turn into a greased baking dish. Bake at 350° for 30 minutes.

Sauté the onions and mushrooms in the margarine until tender. Add the tomato sauce and stir well. Uncover the salmon loaf after cooking for 30 minutes and add the sauce. Cover and continue to cook for an additional 15 to 20 minutes.

Serves 6.

Per serving: 239 calories, 29% of calories from fat, 2.57 gm fiber, 34.7 mg cholesterol, 697 mg sodium, 7.85 gm fat, 1.18 gm saturated fat, 2.86 gm polyunsaturated fat, 1.99 gm monounsaturated fat.

Tuna-Potato Bake

3 7-ounce cans tuna
1 3-ounce can sliced mushrooms
1 tablespoon Wor-
  cestershire sauce
½ teaspoon Tabasco sauce
  .   .   .
2 tablespoons vinegar
3 cups diced, cooked po-
  tatoes
  .   .   .
¼ cup cholesterol-free margarine
¼ cup thinly sliced onion
¼ cup thinly sliced celery
¼ cup all-purpose flour
3 tablespoons oat bran
1 teaspoon dry mustard
2 cups skim milk
1 cup plain nonfat yogurt

Combine the tuna, mushrooms, Worcestershire sauce, and Tabasco sauce, and set aside. Combine the vinegar and potatoes in a separate bowl and set aside. Melt the margarine in a sauté pan and simmer the onion and celery until tender. Add the flour, oat bran, and dry mustard, and remove from the heat. Gradually add the milk and yogurt, stirring until well blended. Place half of the potatoes in a large casserole. Top with half of the tuna mixture and half of the sauce mixture. Repeat the layers. Bake at 350° for 35 minutes.

Serves 6.

Per serving: 333 calories, 28% of calories from fat, 4.33 gm fiber, 180 mg cholesterol, 126 mg sodium, 26.7 gm fat, 10.7 gm saturated fat, 1.08 gm polyunsaturated fat, 11.7 gm monounsaturated fat.

SIDE DISHES

Apple-Carrot Casserole

1 teaspoon lemon juice
1 teaspoon brown sugar
½ teaspoon ground ginger
½ teaspoon cinnamon
½ cup water
2 apples, pared, cored and
   chopped
6 carrots, grated
¾ cup oat bran
2 egg whites, slightly beaten

    •   •   •

Oat Bran Croutons (see
   recipe on p. 72)

Combine the lemon juice, brown sugar, ginger, cinnamon, and water in a bowl. Add the apples, carrots, and oat bran. Stir in the egg whites. Pour into an oiled or sprayed casserole dish and top with croutons. Bake covered at 350° for 30 minutes. Uncover and bake an additional 5 to 10 minutes. (Be careful not to blacken the croutons.)
   Serves 8.

Per serving: 122 calories, 21% of calories from fat, 4.47 gm fiber, 4.29 mg cholesterol, 52.2 mg sodium, 3.10 gm fat, 0.38 gm saturated fat, 1.07 gm polyunsaturated fat, 0.68 gm monounsaturated fat.

Baked Broccoli

1 10-ounce package frozen chopped broccoli

1 10¾-ounce can reduced sodium cream of mushroom soup

½ cup plain lowfat yogurt

1 egg or egg substitute equivalent

1 small onion, finely chopped

1 cup shredded low cholesterol imitation Cheddar cheese

1 cup oat bran

¼ cup cholesterol-free margarine

Prepare the broccoli according to the package directions. Drain and combine with the soup, yogurt, egg substitute, onion, and cheese. Place in a 2-quart casserole. Toss the oat bran with the melted margarine and spoon over the broccoli mixture. Bake at 350° for 30 to 35 minutes.
Serves 8.

Per serving: 195 calories, 51% of calories from fat, 3.92 gm fiber, 43.2 mg cholesterol, 179 mg sodium, 11.7 gm fat, 2.81 gm saturated fat, 2.70 gm polyunsaturated fat, 3.03 gm monounsaturated fat.

Black-Eyed Peas and Wild Rice

1 cup uncooked wild rice
2 cups water
1 tablespoon soy sauce
1 bunch green onions,
chopped
1 cube vegetable bouillon

. . .

1 10-ounce package frozen
black-eyed peas
2 tablespoons cholesterol-
free margarine
2 tablespoons oat bran

Bring the rice, water, soy sauce, onions, and bouillon to a boil. Reduce the heat and simmer for 20 minutes. Add the peas and margarine, return to a boil. Reduce the heat and add the oat bran. Cook for an additional 15 to 20 minutes.
Serves 4.

Per serving: 217 calories, 27% of calories from fat, 2.14 gm fiber, 0.04 mg cholesterol, 554 mg sodium, 6.74 gm fat, 1.12 gm saturated fat, 2.47 gm polyunsaturated fat, 2.08 gm monounsaturated fat.

Herbed Broccoli

3 pounds broccoli
2 chicken bouillon cubes
½ cup chopped onion
1 teaspoon minced garlic
1 teaspoon marjoram
1 bay leaf
½ teaspoon Mrs. Dash sea-
soning
3 tablespoons cholesterol-
free margarine, melted

Wash the broccoli and remove the leaves. Place the broccoli in a large stock pot and cover with water. Bring the water to a boil. Add all of the ingredients except the margarine. Cook covered for 10 to 15 minutes or until tender. Drain and drizzle the margarine over the broccoli.
Serves 6.

Per serving: 120 calories, 42% of calories from fat, 8.40 gm fiber, 0.05 mg cholesterol, 427 mg sodium, 6.58 gm fat, 1.13 gm saturated fat, 2.86 gm polyunsaturated fat, 2.10 gm monounsaturated fat.

Creole Cabbage

5 cups chopped cabbage
2 tablespoons cholesterol-
  free margarine
1 large onion, chopped
1 green pepper, chopped
1 1-pound can tomatoes
1 teaspoon sugar
Pepper to taste
1 teaspoon minced garlic
1 cup shredded imitation
  sharp Cheddar cheese

Cook the cabbage in water for 10 minutes. Drain well. Melt the margarine in a large skillet and sauté the onions and green pepper. Add the tomatoes with juice, sugar, pepper, and garlic, and simmer for 5 minutes or more. Combine the cabbage and the tomato mixture in a casserole dish. Sprinkle with cheese and bake at 325° for about 20 minutes or until the cheese melts.
    Serves 4.

Per serving: 220 calories, 43% of calories from fat, 5.44 gm fiber, 16.2 mg cholesterol, 417 mg sodium, 11.1 gm fat, 4.01 gm saturated fat, 2.96 gm polyunsaturated fat, 3.42 gm monounsaturated fat.

Baked Carrots

1 tablespoon minced onion
2 tablespoons cholesterol-
  free margarine
2½ cups mashed, cooked
  carrots
2 cups milk
½ cup minced celery
Dash of pepper
1 cup Oat Bran Bread
  crumbs (see recipe on
  p. 55)
3 egg whites

Sauté the onions in margarine until translucent and tender. Add the mashed carrots. Slowly stir in the milk, celery, seasoning, and bread crumbs. Beat the egg whites and fold into the mixture. Place in a greased baking dish and bake at 350° for 40 minutes.
    Serves 6.

Per serving: 128 calories, 37% of calories from fat, 1.20 gm fiber, 5.31 mg cholesterol, 138 mg sodium, 5.45 gm fat, 0.96 gm saturated fat, 2.30 gm polyunsaturated fat, 1.78 gm monounsaturated fat.

Pureed Carrots

1 cup low-sodium chicken
    broth
4 cups sliced carrots (about
    8 carrots)
¾ cup oat bran
½ cup skim milk
2 tablespoons brown sugar
1 tablespoon safflower oil
½ teaspoon cinnamon
⅛ teaspoon nutmeg
2 tablespoons chopped
    pecans

Bring the broth to a boil in a large saucepan. Add the carrots, cover and simmer for 10 minutes, until tender. Remove from the heat and pour the carrot mixture into a food processor and pulsate in 5 second intervals until smooth. Add the oat bran, milk, sugar, oil, cinnamon, and nutmeg, and mix well. Transfer to a serving bowl and sprinkle with chopped pecans.
Serves 4.

Per serving: 370 calories, 53% of calories from fat, 8.59 gm fiber, 0.5 mg cholesterol, 81.6 mg sodium, 23.6 gm fat, 2.04 gm saturated fat, 5.92 gm polyunsaturated fat, 12.9 gm monounsaturated fat.

Cauliflower au Gratin

1 head cauliflower

2 tablespoons cholesterol-
    free margarine
½ teaspoon white pepper
¼ cup chopped onion
¼ cup oat bran
1 cup skim milk
1½ cups shredded imitation
    Cheddar cheese

Wash the cauliflower and remove the leaves. Break into flowerets. Steam for 5 to 10 minutes, until slightly tender. Drain and place in a greased 2-quart casserole dish. Combine the margarine, pepper, onion, oat bran and milk. Pour over the cauliflower and top with the Cheddar cheese. Bake at 350° for 35 to 40 minutes.
Serves 6.

Per serving: 149 calories, 51% of calories from fat, 2.18 gm fiber, 16.9 mg cholesterol, 214 mg sodium, 8.84 gm fat, 3.62 gm saturated fat, 2.25 gm polyunsaturated fat, 2.67 gm monounsaturated fat.

Cheesy Scalloped Cucumbers

3 slices Oat Bran Bread
   (see recipe on p. 55)
3 large cucumbers, peeled
   and sliced ⅓ to ½ inch
   thick
Salt substitute to taste
Pepper to taste
2 tablespoons minced onion
½ cup cholesterol-free margarine
¾ cup skim milk
½ cup grated imitation
   sharp Cheddar cheese

Crumble the bread into a greased baking dish. Place about half the cucumber slices over the bread crumbs and sprinkle with salt substitute and pepper, and a small amount of minced onion. Add a little margarine. Repeat the layers of cucumber and seasonings. Pour the milk over the layers. Sprinkle the top with Cheddar cheese. Bake at 350° for 30 minutes or until browned.
   Serves 6.

Per serving: 273 calories, 65% of calories from fat, 4.05 gm fiber, 15.1 mg cholesterol, 291 mg sodium, 20.4 gm fat, 4.13 gm saturated fat, 8.14 gm polyunsaturated fat, 6.74 gm monounsaturated fat.

Eggplant Parmigiana

1 medium eggplant
2 tomatoes, chopped
⅔ cup tomato juice
½ cup old-fashioned rolled
   oats
½ cup oat bran
1 teaspoon dried basil
¼ teaspoon dried oregano
2 cloves garlic, minced
½ cup grated reduced-fat
   Mozzarella cheese
2 tablespoons Parmesan
   cheese

Cut the stem off the eggplant and slice lengthwise in ½-inch strips. Place in a greased 8-inch square baking dish, overlapping the strips. Combine the tomatoes, tomato juice, oats, oat bran, spices, and garlic. Spread over the eggplant. Sprinkle with Mozzarella cheese and top with Parmesan cheese. Bake at 350° for 45 to 50 minutes.
   Serves 4.

Per serving: 159 calories, 25% of calories from fat, 6.44 gm fiber, 10.6 mg cholesterol, 279 mg sodium, 4.85 gm fat, 2.12 gm saturated fat, 0.26 gm polyunsaturated fat, 0.97 gm monounsaturated fat.

Stuffed Eggplant

1 large eggplant
½ cup water
½ teaspoon salt substitute
. . .

¼ cup chopped onion
1 tablespoon cholesterol-
free margarine
1 10½-ounce can reduced-
sodium cream of mush-
room soup
1 teaspoon Worcestershire
sauce
1 cup oat bran
1 tablespoon chopped par-
sley
. . .

1½ cups water

Slice off and discard one side of the eggplant. Remove the pulp to within ½ inch of the skin. Dice the pulp and place in a saucepan. Add the water and salt. Simmer until the eggplant is tender. Drain. Sauté the onion in margarine until golden brown. Combine the onion, mushroom soup, Worcestershire sauce and all of the oat bran except 2 tablespoons into the eggplant pulp. Fill the eggplant shell with the mixture. Place the eggplant in a shallow baking pan. Sprinkle the top with the reserved oat bran and the parsley. Pour 1½ cups of water into the baking pan around the eggplant. Bake at 375° for 1 hour, until piping hot.
Serves 4.

Per serving: 181 calories, 36% of calories from fat, 6.48 gm fiber, 0.00 mg cholesterol, 68.9 mg sodium, 8.20 gm fat, 0.55 gm saturated fat, 1.35 gm polyunsaturated fat, 1.04 gm monounsaturated fat.

Cajun Green Beans

1 pound fresh green beans
Water as needed
½ cup chopped green pep-
   per
½ cup chopped celery
½ cup chopped onion
2 tablespoons cholesterol-
   free margarine
1 tablespoon chopped pi-
   miento
⅓ cup chili sauce
1 teaspoon paprika

Cook the beans in water until tender and drain. Sauté the green pepper, celery, and onion in margarine until tender. Add the pimiento, chili sauce, paprika and green beans. Stir until just heated through.
   Serves 6.

Per serving: 59 calories, 29% of calories from fat, 1.63 gm fiber, 0.00 mg cholesterol, 221 mg sodium, 2.08 gm fat, 0.36 gm saturated fat, 0.91 gm polyunsaturated fat, 0.69 gm monounsaturated fat.

French Green Bean and Rice Casserole

2 small or 1 large onion,
   chopped
2 tablespoons cholesterol-
   free margarine
½ cup rice, uncooked
1 1-pound can tomatoes
1 16-ounce can French-style
   green beans
⅛ teaspoon pepper
⅓ cup water
1 teaspoon Mrs. Dash sea-
   soning

Sauté the onions in margarine until brown. Add the rice, tomatoes, green beans, water, and seasoning. Simmer for 30 minutes.
   Serves 4.

Per serving: 218 calories, 26% of calories from fat, 4.49 gm fiber, 0.00 mg cholesterol, 548 mg sodium, 6.53 gm fat, 1.12 gm saturated fat, 2.74 gm polyunsaturated fat, 2.11 gm monounsaturated fat.

Baked Italian Onions

6 whole onions
6 tablespoons Italian salad
   dressing
Parmesan cheese
¼ cup oat bran

Peel and wash the onions. Slice off the tops and bottoms evenly so they sit straight. Score each onion in a crosswise fashion leaving the outer ring intact. Place each onion in an aluminum foil square that has been coated with vegetable spray. Pull the foil up around the onion leaving the top open and exposed, tulip-fashioned. Spoon one tablespoon of salad dressing over each onion. Combine the Parmesan and oat bran and sprinkle over the top of each onion. Bake at 350° for 1 hour.
   Serves 6.

Per serving: 254 calories, 33% of calories from fat, 8.07 gm fiber, 3.29 mg cholesterol, 203 mg sodium, 9.80 gm fat, 2.00 gm saturated fat, 4.59 gm polyunsaturated fat, 2.23 gm monounsaturated fat.

Cheesy Whipped Potatoes

3 pounds potatoes, cooked,
   peeled, and whipped
½ cup cholesterol-free margarine
6 ounces lowfat cottage
   cheese
1 green pepper, chopped
¼ cup oat bran
½ cup grated imitation
   Cheddar cheese
¼ cup grated Parmesan
   cheese

Whip the potatoes with the margarine, cottage cheese, pepper, oat bran, and Cheddar cheese. Place in a baking dish and top with Parmesan. Bake at 350° for 30 minutes or until golden brown.
   Serves 6.

Per serving: 425 calories, 39% of calories from fat, 6.15 gm fiber, 9.95 mg cholesterol, 453 mg sodium, 18.9 gm fat, 4.62 gm saturated fat, 6.76 gm polyunsaturated fat, 6.28 gm monounsaturated fat.

Stuffed Baked Potatoes

6 Idaho baking potatoes

½ cup cholesterol-free margarine
1 tablespoon minced onion
1 cup plain lowfat yogurt
Paprika to taste
Pepper to taste
¼ cup oat bran

Bake the potatoes until tender. Split them lengthwise and scoop the potatoes out of the skins, reserving the shells. While they are still hot, whip the potatoes with the margarine, onion, yogurt, and seasonings. Spoon the mixture back into the shells. Sprinkle the tops with the oat bran. Return to the oven and bake at 350° for an additional 10 minutes.
   Serves 12.

Per serving: 159 calories, 45% of calories from fat, 2.16 gm fiber, 1.17 mg cholesterol, 119 mg sodium, 8.13 gm fat, 1.51 gm saturated fat, 3.32 gm polyunsaturated fat, 2.78 gm monounsaturated fat.

Scalloped Potatoes

2½ cups skim milk
6 medium potatoes, peeled
    and sliced
¼ cup diced onion
¼ cup diced celery
Paprika
3 tablespoons all-purpose
    flour
3 tablespoons oat bran
3 tablespoons plain lowfat
    yogurt
⅛ teaspoon pepper
Parmesan cheese
2 tablespoons cholesterol-
    free margarine

Scald the skim milk in a saucepan. Set aside and allow to cool to lukewarm. Place a layer of cut-up potatoes in the bottom on a baking pan. Sprinkle the top of the potatoes with half the onion, celery, and paprika.

Combine the lukewarm milk, flour, oat bran, yogurt, and pepper. Pour a thin layer over the first layer of potatoes and sprinkle with Parmesan. Top with the remaining potatoes, celery, and onion, and sprinkle with paprika. Add the remaining milk mixture and sprinkle with Parmesan. Dot the top of the potatoes with margarine. Cover and bake at 350° for 30 minutes. Uncover and bake for an additional 50 minutes or until the potatoes are tender.

Serves 8.

Per serving: 191 calories, 18% of calories from fat, 3.32 gm fiber, 2.81 mg cholesterol, 120 mg sodium, 3.86 gm fat, 0.97 gm saturated fat, 1.30 gm polyunsaturated fat, 1.21 gm monounsaturated fat.

Broiled Tomatoes

5 tomatoes
½ cup oat bran
½ cup grated Parmesan
   cheese
⅛ cup minced parsley
¼ cup cholesterol-free margarine, melted

Slice the tomatoes ½-inch thick and discard the ends. Place on a broiler pan. Combine the remaining ingredients and place an equal portion of the mixture on the top of each tomato. Broil for 5 minutes, until hot. Serve immediately.
   Serves 6 to 8.

Per serving: 140 calories, 65% of calories from fat, 2.46 gm fiber, 6.58 mg cholesterol, 266 mg sodium, 10.6 gm fat, 2.93 gm saturated fat, 3.43 gm polyunsaturated fat, 3.46 gm monounsaturated fat.

Spaghetti Squash and Vegetables

1 medium spaghetti squash

6 to 8 large tomatoes, cut
   up
1 large onion, coarsely
   chopped
½ cup oat bran
1 tablespoon Italian seasoning
2 cups mixed cooked vege-
   tables such as broccoli,
   cauliflower, and carrots

Split the spaghetti squash in half. Scoop out the seeds and place cut side down on a greased baking sheet. Bake at 350° for 35 to 45 minutes. Scoop the pulp out with a fork into spaghetti-like strands. Drain if needed. Set aside.
   Combine the tomatoes, onion, oat bran flakes, and Italian seasoning. Bring to a boil and then reduce to a simmer in a large pot. Cook for approximately 25 minutes. Before serving, add the cooked vegetables to the sauce and serve over the spaghetti.
   Serves 8.

Per serving: 72.6 calories, 9% of calories from fat, 4.83 gm fiber, 0.00 mg cholesterol, 18.4 mg sodium, 0.83 gm fat, 0.11 gm saturated fat, 0.31 gm polyunsaturated fat, 0.07 gm monounsaturated fat.

Summer Squash Casserole

3 to 4 medium yellow squash, sliced about ¼-inch thick
3 medium tomatoes, sliced about ¼ inch thick
½ cup thinly sliced onions
½ cup plain lowfat yogurt
⅓ cup shredded imitation sharp Cheddar cheese
⅓ cup oat bran
2 teaspoons Mrs. Dash seasoning

Layer half of the vegetables in a greased 2-quart casserole dish. In the middle layer add the yogurt. Combine the cheese, oat bran, and seasonings. Sprinkle half of the cheese mixture over the vegetables. Top with the remaining vegetables, and the remaining cheese mixture. Bake at 350° for 30 minutes.

Serves 6.

Per serving: 155 calories, 17% of calories from fat, 10.0 gm fiber, 5.49 mg cholesterol, 59.6 mg sodium, 3.43 gm fat, 1.28 gm saturated fat, 0.71 gm polyunsaturated fat, 0.56 gm monounsaturated fat.

Oat Bran Zucchini Casserole

1 pound zucchini, unpeeled

1 tablespoon safflower oil
½ cup chopped onion
1 large clove garlic, minced

2 egg whites, beaten
2 cups tomato sauce
1 teaspoon dried basil
¼ teaspoon freshly ground
  black pepper
1 cup oat bran
½ cup shredded reduced-fat
  Mozzarella cheese
Parmesan cheese

Grate the zucchini in a food processor and place in a collander to drain. In hot oil, sauté the onions and garlic until the onions are tender and transparent. Add the zucchini, stirring until coated with oil. Combine the egg whites, tomato sauce, basil, pepper, and oat bran in a large bowl. Add the zucchini mixture and pour into a baking dish. Sprinkle the top with Mozzarella and Parmesan. Bake at 350° for 35 to 40 minutes.

Serves 6.

Per serving: 145 calories, 32% of calories from fat, 3.44 gm fiber, 7.05 mg cholesterol, 596 mg sodium, 5.69 gm fat, 1.75 gm saturated fat, 1.03 gm polyunsaturated fat, 1.63 gm monounsaturated fat.

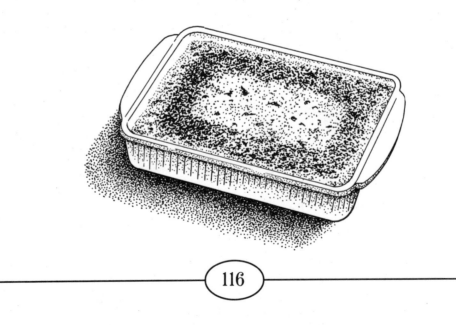

Zucchini au Gratin

4 large zucchini, sliced ½
  inch thick
1 cup shredded reduced-
  cholesterol imitation
  Cheddar cheese
⅓ cup skim milk
½ cup plain lowfat yogurt
¼ cup oat bran

Arrange the zucchini in a casserole dish. Mix ½ cup of the cheese, the skim milk, and yogurt together and pour over the zucchini. Sprinkle the top with the remaining cheese and oat bran. Bake at 350° for 40 to 45 minutes, or until the zucchini is easily pierced with a fork and the top of the casserole is lightly browned.
Serves 8.

Per serving: 119 calories, 20% of calories from fat, 5.48 gm fiber, 9.13 mg cholesterol, 90.3 mg sodium, 2.94 gm fat, 1.65 gm saturated fat, 0.16 gm polyunsaturated fat, 0.73 gm monounsaturated fat.

Zucchini Casserole

5 or 6 zucchini squash
3 ounces plain lowfat yogurt
⅛ teaspoon garlic powder
⅛ cup minced onion
½ cup Oat Bran Bread
  crumbs (see recipe on
  p. 55)
Parmesan cheese
Paprika to taste

Slice the zucchini into 2-inch pieces, and cook in small amount of boiling water for 8 to 10 minutes. Drain well, and add the yogurt, garlic, and onion. Place in a greased casserole dish and top with the bread crumbs and Parmesan cheese. Sprinkle with paprika. Bake at 350° for 30 minutes.
Serves 6.

Per serving: 202 calories, 18% of calories from fat, 10.4 gm fiber, 11.3 mg cholesterol, 104 mg sodium, 4.44 gm fat, 1.22 gm saturated fat, 1.48 gm polyunsaturated fat, 1.14 gm monounsaturated fat.

Macaroni and Cheese

1½ cups skim milk
1½ tablespoons oat bran
1½ tablespoons cholesterol-
   free margarine
¾ cup grated lowfat Amer-
   ican cheese

•   •   •

2 cups macaroni, cooked
   and drained

•   •   •

¼ cup cheese cracker
   crumbs
Pepper
Paprika

Combine the milk, oat bran, and margarine. Cook over low heat to make a white sauce. Add the cheese, stirring constantly. Cook until the cheese has melted and the sauce boils. Remove from the heat. Alternate layers of macaroni and cheese sauce in a nonstick baking dish and cover the top with cheese cracker crumbs. Sprinkle with pepper and paprika to taste. Bake at 375° until the mixture bubbles and the crumbs brown.
Serves 6.

Per serving: 151 calories, 30% of calories from fat, 0.61 gm fiber, 9.10 mg cholesterol, 160 mg sodium, 5.02 gm fat, 1.99 gm saturated fat, 0.72 gm polyunsaturated fat, 1.20 gm monounsaturated fat.

Golden Mediterranean Pilaf

3 cups low sodium chicken
   broth
1½ cups uncooked long
   grain white rice
4 tablespoons vegetable oil
½ cup seedless golden raisins
½ teaspoon turmeric
½ teaspoon curry powder
1 tablespoon soy sauce

Bring the chicken broth to a boil in a 1-quart saucepan. In another medium saucepan, combine the rice, oil, raisins, turmeric, curry and soy sauce. Pour the chicken broth over the rice mixture. Cover and cook over low heat for 20 minutes or until all of the liquid is absorbed and the rice is tender.
Serves 8.

Per serving: 226 calories, 30% of calories from fat, 1.15 gm fiber, 0.00 mg cholesterol, 151 mg sodium, 7.62 gm fat, 1.05 gm saturated fat, 2.58 gm polyunsaturated fat, 2.93 gm monounsaturated fat.

Orange Curried Rice and Mushrooms

¼ cup cholesterol-free margarine
½ cup chopped onion
½ cup sliced mushrooms
2 teaspoons curry powder
1 cup uncooked wild rice
1 cup orange juice
1 cup chicken broth

Sauté the onions and mushrooms in the margarine until soft. Add the curry powder and rice and cook and stir for 2 minutes. Add the remaining ingredients and stir with a fork. Bring to a boil. Reduce the heat; cover, and simmer for 20 minutes.
Serves 6.

Per serving: 209 calories, 35% of calories from fat, 0.91 gm fiber, 0.17 mg cholesterol, 219 mg sodium, 8 gm fat, 1.59 gm saturated fat, 2.46 gm polyunsaturated fat, 3.46 gm monounsaturated fat.

Oriental Oat Bran Pilaf

1 tablespoon cholesterol-free margarine
1 cup sliced mushrooms
½ cup chopped red pepper
½ cup sliced green onions
½ cup chopped celery
1 cup rolled oats
¾ cup oat bran
2 egg whites
2 tablespoons soy sauce
1 cup chicken broth
1 6-ounce package frozen pea pods, thawed

Melt the margarine over medium heat. Add the mushrooms, pepper, onion and celery and sauté for 2 to 3 minutes. Combine the oats, oat bran, egg whites, and soy sauce in a separate bowl. Coat all of the oat bran well, then add the mixture to the vegetable mixture. Cook for an additional 5 minutes or until lightly browned. Add the chicken broth and pea pods and cook until the liquid is absorbed and the vegetables are tender.
Serves 4.

Per serving: 205 calories, 24% of calories from fat, 5.75 gm fiber, 0.25 mg cholesterol, 788 mg sodium, 6.13 gm fat, 0.63 gm saturated fat, 1.40 gm polyunsaturated fat, 1.18 gm monounsaturated fat.

DESSERTS

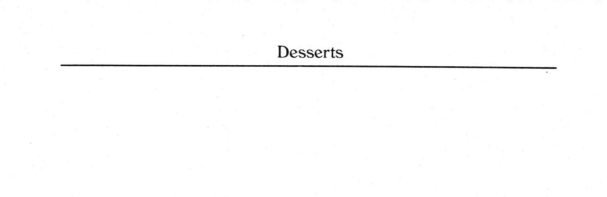

Applesauce Oat Cake

¾ cup cholesterol-free margarine

¾ cup cholesterol-free oil

4 tablespoons sugar

1 teaspoon baking powder

¼ teaspoon baking soda

1 cup unsweetened applesauce or freshly peeled apples that have been pureed in a food processor

2 cups all-purpose flour

1 cup oat bran

2 egg whites

1 teaspoon cinnamon

¼ teaspoon nutmeg

⅛ teaspoon ground cloves

¾ cup raisins

¼ cup chopped nuts

1 teaspoon vanilla extract

Combine all of the ingredients and mix well. Pour into a greased bundt pan and bake at 350° for 1 to 1½ hours or until done (cake springs back when touched).

Serves 12.

Per serving: 390 calories, 61% of calories from fat, 2.74 gm fiber, 0.00 mg cholesterol, 209 mg sodium, 27.3 gm fat, 4.13 gm saturated fat, 11.0 gm polyunsaturated fat, 10.3 gm monounsaturated fat.

Carrot Cake

1½ cups sifted unbleached
   all-purpose flour
2 teaspoons baking powder
½ teaspoon baking soda
1 teaspoon cinnamon
¼ teaspoon ground cloves
¼ cup sugar

⅔ cup safflower oil
4 egg whites

1 cup old-fashioned rolled
   oats
¾ cup oat bran

1 cup finely grated carrots
⅓ cup chopped walnuts
⅓ cup raisins

Blend together the flour, baking powder, soda, cinnamon, cloves, and sugar. Add the oil and egg whites, and mix well. Add the rolled oats and oat bran. Stir well. Stir in the carrots, walnuts, and raisins. Spread into a 9 x 13-inch baking pan. Bake at 350° for 40 minutes. Serve topped with a non-dairy whipped topping.

Serves 12.

Per serving: 264 calories, 49% of calories from fat, 1.86 gm fiber, 0.00 mg cholesterol, 112 mg sodium, 15.1 gm fat, 1.97 gm saturated fat, 5.82 gm polyunsaturated fat, 5.63 gm monounsaturated fat.

Classic Sugar-Free Fruitcake

½ cup rum
1 6-ounce can frozen orange juice concentrate, thawed
1 cup chopped cranberries

• • •

1 8-ounce package chopped, pitted dates
1 cup chopped pecans
1 tablespoon grated orange rind
1 tablespoon vanilla extract
2 eggs, lightly beaten (egg substitute can be used)
1 8-ounce can unsweetened pineapple tidbits, drained

• • •

2 cups all-purpose flour
¼ cup oat bran
1¼ teaspoons baking soda
½ teaspoon cinnamon
½ teaspoon nutmeg
¼ teaspoon allspice

• • •

½ cup rum
½ cup orange juice

Combine ½ cup of rum, orange juice concentrate, chopped cranberries and set aside to stand for 1 hour. Combine the dates, pecans, orange rind, vanilla, eggs, and pineapple. Add to the cranberry mixture and stir. Combine the flour, oat bran, baking soda, and spices. Add to the fruit mixture and stir well. Spoon the batter into a greased bundt pan. Bake at 325° for 45 minutes or until a toothpick inserted in the center comes out clean. Remove from pan when it has cooled for 20 minutes. Place several layers of cheesecloth over the top of the cake. Pour ½ cup of rum and the orange juice over the cheesecloth. Wrap the cake and cheesecloth in wax or plastic wrap and then in foil and store in a cool dry place for 1 week.

Serves 16.

Per serving: 220 calories, 22% of calories from fat, 2.70 gm fiber, 34.3 mg cholesterol, 73.8 mg sodium, 5.62 gm fat, 0.61 gm saturated fat, 1.23 gm polyunsaturated fat, 3.13 gm monounsaturated fat.

Gingerbread

¾ cup oat bran
¾ cup rolled oats
1½ cups fine whole wheat
flour
¼ cup sugar
1 teaspoon ground ginger
1 teaspoon baking powder

2 tablespoons molasses
2 tablespoons cholesterol-
free margarine
1 cup lowfat buttermilk, or
skim milk
1 tablespoon grated orange
rind
2 egg whites, beaten

Mix together the oat bran, oats, and flour in a large mixing bowl. Stir in the sugar, ginger, and baking powder. Heat the molasses and margarine in a saucepan until warm. Stir in the buttermilk, orange rind, and egg whites. Stir the oat bran mixture into the molasses mixture. Beat well. Pour the batter into a baking pan. Bake at 350° for 50 minutes or until center of cake tests clean with a toothpick. Cool in the pan for 15 minutes. Remove the gingerbread to a wire rack to finish cooling. Wrap and refrigerate before serving.
Serves 16.

Per serving: 104 calories, 18% of calories from fat, 2.04 gm fiber, 0.25 mg cholesterol, 55.1 mg sodium, 2.24 gm fat, 0.30 gm saturated fat, 0.62 gm polyunsaturated fat, 0.51 gm monounsaturated fat.

Old-Fashioned Apple Cake

1¼ cups sifted unbleached
　all-purpose flour
1 teaspoon baking powder
1 teaspoon baking soda
1 teaspoon cinnamon
½ teaspoon nutmeg
½ cup brown sugar

    •   •   •

¾ cup oat bran
½ cup rolled oats
½ cup chopped walnuts
4 egg whites
⅓ cup unsweetened orange
　juice
2 tablespoons vegetable oil

    •   •   •

1½ cups peeled and shred-
　ded apples
　(approximately 2 medium
　sized apples)

Blend together the flour, baking powder, soda, cinnamon, nutmeg, and brown sugar. Stir in the oat bran, oats, walnuts, egg whites, orange juice, and oil. Fold in the shredded apples. Pour into a sprayed 9 x 13" baking pan or a bundt pan. Bake at 350° for 45 minutes or until a toothpick inserted in the center comes out clean.

Serves 12.

Per serving: 182 calories, 29% of calories from fat, 1.57 gm fiber, 0.00 mg cholesterol, 117 mg sodium, 6.20 gm fat, 0.64 gm saturated fat, 2.83 gm polyunsaturated fat, 1.69 gm monounsaturated fat.

Apple and Apricot Oat Pie

Pie Filling:
¼ cup sugar
2 tablespoons cornstarch
2 tablespoons oat bran
2 tablespoons grated lemon
    rind
3 tablespoons orange juice
1 teaspoon cinnamon
½ teaspoon nutmeg
1 cup chopped apricots
8 large apples, peeled,
    cored, and sliced

.   .   .

1 Oat Bran Pie Crust (see
    recipe on p. 131)

.   .   .

Streusel:
½ cup all-purpose flour
1 teaspoon cinnamon
½ cup cholesterol-free mar-
    garine
¼ cup sugar

Combine ¼ cup of sugar, cornstarch, oat bran, lemon rind, orange juice, 1 teaspoon of cinnamon, and nutmeg. Mix thoroughly. Add the fruit and toss until well coated. Pour into the uncooked pastry shell. Combine the remaining ingredients and sprinkle over the pie. Bake at 425° for 15 minutes, then decrease the oven temperature to 350° and bake for an additional 45 minutes.

Serves 8.

Per serving: 421 calories, 40% of calories from fat, 7.45 gm fiber, 0.00 mg cholesterol, 156 mg sodium, 19.9 gm fat, 3.10 gm saturated fat, 7.64 gm polyunsaturated fat, 7.05 gm monounsaturated fat.

Dutch Peach Pie

Pie Filling:
6-ounce can frozen orange juice concentrate, thawed
¾ cup water
⅛ teaspoon allspice
⅛ teaspoon cinnamon
2 tablespoons oat bran
1 tablespoon cornstarch
¼ cup brown sugar
12 peaches, peeled and sliced

* * *

1 Oat Bran Pie Crust (see recipe on p. 131)

Streusel:
½ cup all-purpose flour
1 teaspoon cinnamon
½ cup cholesterol-free margarine
¼ cup sugar

Combine the orange juice, water, allspice, ⅛ teaspoon cinnamon, oat bran, cornstarch, and brown sugar in a large bowl. Mix well. Add the peaches and gently stir until well combined. Pour into the uncooked pie shell.

Combine the remaining ingredients and sprinkle over the pie. Bake at 425° for 15 minutes. Reduce the temperature to 350° and bake an additional 45 minutes.

Serves 8.

Per serving: 413 calories, 40% of calories from fat, 6.67 gm fiber, 0.00 mg cholesterol, 158 mg sodium, 19.4 gm fat, 3.03 gm saturated fat, 7.54 gm polyunsaturated fat, 7.03 gm monounsaturated fat.

Pumpkin Pie

1 whole egg plus 4 egg
whites
1 16-ounce can pumpkin
½ cup brown sugar
⅓ cup honey
¼ cup oat bran
1 teaspoon cinnamon
1 12-ounce can skim evaporated milk
½ teaspoon ginger
⅛ teaspoon ground cloves
½ teaspoon vanilla extract

• • •

Oat Bran Pie Crust (see
recipe on p. 131)

Mix all of the ingredients well in a large bowl. Pour into an uncooked oat bran pie shell. Bake at 425° for 15 minutes and then lower the oven temperature to 350°. Continue to cook for 45 minutes. The pie is done when a knife inserted in the center comes out clean.

Serves 6.

Per serving: 414 calories, 24% of calories from fat, 4.72 gm fiber, 48.0 mg cholesterol, 122 mg sodium, 11.7 gm fat, 1.84 gm saturated fat, 3.55 gm polyunsaturated fat, 4.34 gm monounsaturated fat.

Apple-Cranberry Cobbler

3 cups peeled, chopped
   cooking apples
2 cups cranberries
¼ cup fructose
¼ cup apple juice
¼ cup all-purpose flour
1 tablespoon lemon juice
1 teaspoon cinnamon
½ teaspoon nutmeg

•　　•　　•

½ cup cholesterol-free margarine
1½ cups uncooked oatmeal
⅓ cup all-purpose flour
½ cup chopped pecans

Combine the apples, cranberries, fructose, apple juice, ¼ cup of flour, the lemon juice, and spices. Set aside.

Combine the margarine, oatmeal, flour and pecans. Press into the bottom and sides of a pie plate, reserving ¼ cup of the mixture. Add the apple and cranberry mixture. Sprinkle the top with the reserved oatmeal mixture and bake at 350° for 45 minutes. The cobbler should be bubbly when done.

Serves 8.

Per serving: 306 calories, 49% of calories from fat, 2.06 gm fiber, 0.00 mg cholesterol, 154 mg sodium, 17.4 gm fat, 2.36 gm saturated fat, 6.09 gm polyunsaturated fat, 6.89 gm monounsaturated fat.

Oat Bran Pie Crust

1 cup whole wheat flour
½ cup oat bran
¼ cup safflower oil
3 tablespoons sugar-free
   lemon lime soda

Combine the flour and bran. Stir in the oil and crumble by hand while adding the soda. Form into a ball and roll out between two sheets of wax paper. Press the dough in a lightly greased pie pan and prick with a fork.

Makes one pie crust, or 8 slices.

Per serving: 137 calories, 47% of calories from fat, 3.13 gm fiber, 0.00 mg cholesterol, 1.56 mg sodium, 7.66 gm fat, 1.04 gm saturated fat, 2.56 gm polyunsaturated fat, 2.93 gm monounsaturated fat.

Fruit Topping

1 cup old-fashioned rolled
  oats
¾ cup oat bran
1 cup wheat bran
2 tablespoons shelled sunflower seeds
2 tablespoons sesame
  seeds
2 tablespoons chopped walnuts
½ cup chopped dates
1 teaspoon cinnamon

Mix all of the ingredients together in a large mixing bowl. The mixture should be crumbly. Place
in an airtight container and keep refrigerated.
This is best served over fresh fruit and lowfat or
nonfat yogurt.
  Serves 16.

*Per serving: 78 calories, 26% of calories from fat, 2.48 gm
fiber, 0.00 mg cholesterol, 29.0 mg sodium, 2.60 gm fat, 0.23
gm saturated fat, 1.10 gm polyunsaturated fat, 0.49 gm
monounsaturated fat.*

Oat Bran Blueberry Crepe

½ cup blueberries, fresh or frozen
1 teaspoon vanilla extract
  •   •   •
1 .035-ounce envelope sugar substitute
  •   •   •
1 egg white
¼ cup plain lowfat yogurt
1 slice Oat Bran Bread, crumbled (see recipe on p. 55)
Pinch ground cinnamon
½ teaspoon vanilla extract
1 teaspoon cholesterol-free margarine

Combine the blueberries and 1 teaspoon of vanilla in a saucepan. Barely cover with water. Bring the berries to a slow boil and cook uncovered over medium heat, stirring often, until the consistency of preserves. Remove the berries from the heat, cover, and cool for 5 minutes. Add the sugar substitute.

Combine the egg white, yogurt, bread, cinnamon, and ½ teaspoon vanilla. Blend until smooth. Heat a 10-inch nonstick skillet over low heat and pour in the blender contents, tilting the pan to spread evenly. Lift the edges with a rubber spatula and turn only when brown-flecked or the pancake may tear. Cook the other side. Spread fruit in the center and roll up. Serve dotted with margarine.

Serves 1.

Per serving: 295 calories, 34% of calories from fat, 5.74 gm fiber, 21.8 mg cholesterol, 196 mg sodium, 11.6 gm fat, 2.16 gm saturated fat, 4.59 gm polyunsaturated fat, 3.38 gm monounsaturated fat.

Blueberry Slump

3 cups blueberries
¼ cup orange juice

· · ·

¼ cup sugar
½ teaspoon cinnamon

· · ·

½ cup all-purpose flour
¼ cup oat bran
2 teaspoons baking powder
1 tablespoon sugar
½ cup skim milk
3 tablespoons cholesterol-
    free margarine, softened

Place the blueberries in a greased casserole dish. Toss with the orange juice. Combine ¼ cup of sugar and the cinnamon, and sprinkle over the blueberries. Combine the flour, oat bran, baking powder, and 1 tablespoon of sugar. Make a well in the center of the dry ingredients and add the skim milk. Work by hand until the mixture resembles coarse crumbs. Add the softened margarine and continue to work by hand. Sprinkle over the blueberries. Bake at 350° for 20 minutes or until golden brown. Serve warm.
Serves 4.

Per serving: 289 calories, 29% of calories from fat, 4.32 gm fiber, 0.50 mg cholesterol, 307 mg sodium, 9.60 gm fat, 1.53 gm saturated fat, 3.69 gm polyunsaturated fat, 3.05 gm monounsaturated fat.

Bread Pudding with Raisins

2 slices day old Oat Bran
  Bread, cubed (see recipe
  on p. 55)
½ cup raisins
2 cups skim milk
½ cup egg substitute
4 tablespoons sugar
1 teaspoon cinnamon
1 teaspoon vanilla extract
¼ teaspoon nutmeg

Mix the bread cubes and raisins in 1½ quart baking dish. Combine the remaining ingredients and pour over the bread and raisins. Stir to combine. Set the dish in a shallow pan on the oven rack. Pour hot water in the pan to a depth of 1 inch. Bake at 350° for 45 to 55 minutes or until a knife inserted in the center comes out clean.
  Serves 4.

Per serving: 251 calories, 16% of calories from fat, 3.47 gm fiber, 11.5 mg cholesterol, 144 mg sodium, 4.67 gm fat, 0.85 gm saturated fat, 2.00 gm polyunsaturated fat, 1.24 gm monounsaturated fat.

Apple Crunch

1 cup rolled oats
½ cup all-purpose flour
1 teaspoon cinnamon
½ cup cholesterol-free margarine

•   •   •

3 cups apples, chopped
1 tablespoon all-purpose
  flour
1 teaspoon cinnamon
1 tablespoon orange juice
¼ cup sugar

Combine the oats, ½ cup of flour, 1 teaspoon of cinnamon, and margarine, and mix until crumbly in texture. Place half of the mixture in the bottom of a baking pan. Combine the apples, 1 tablespoon of flour, 1 teaspoon of cinnamon, juice and the sugar. Place in the pan over the oat mixture. Cover with the remainder of the oat mixture. Bake at 350° for 45 minutes.
  Serves 6.

Per serving: 291 calories, 49% of calories from fat, 1.67 gm fiber, 0.00 mg cholesterol, 204 mg sodium, 16.5 gm fat, 2.66 gm saturated fat, 6.61 gm polyunsaturated fat, 5.40 gm monounsaturated fat.

Cheesy Apples

6 cups pared, sliced apples
1 teaspoon cinnamon
½ cup apple cider
⅓ cup all-purpose flour
¼ cup oat bran
¼ teaspoon salt substitute
½ cup cholesterol-free margarine
¼ cup cheese cracker crumbs
1 cup grated imitation Cheddar cheese

Arrange the apples in a sprayed baking dish. Sprinkle them with cinnamon and cover with the cider. Combine the flour, oat bran, salt substitute, margarine, cracker crumbs and cheese, and mix until the consistency of coarse crumbs. Sprinkle the mixture over the apples. Bake at 350° for 1 hour or until the apples are tender.
Serves 6.

Per serving: 301 calories, 56% of calories from fat, 3.45 gm fiber, 10.8 ng cholesterol, 308 mg sodium, 19.4 gm fat, 4.73 gm saturated fat, 6.76 gm polyunsaturated fat, 6.27 gm monounsaturated fat.

Baked Whole Peaches

1 cup all-purpose flour
½ cup oat bran
1 teaspoon salt substitute
¼ cup cholesterol-free margarine
3 tablespoons cold sugar-free lemon lime soda

•   •   •

In a bowl mix flour, oat bran, salt substitute and margarine until of coarse consistency. Add the soda and mix by hand. Form into a ball and roll out similar to a pie crust. Cut the dough into 4 circles and place an unpeeled peach in the center of each circle of dough. Completely cover the peaches. Seal the peach completely. Combine

4 peaches

1 egg white with 2 table-
 spoons water
Cinnamon to sprinkle

the egg white and water. Place the peaches on a baking dish and brush the top with the egg white mixture. Sprinkle with a small amount of cinnamon. Bake at 400° for 35 to 40 minutes until golden in color and the crust is flaky. The skin of the peach will disappear when cooked. To serve, open the peach with a knife by cutting down the center. Remove the stone and eat.
 Serves 4.

Per serving: 292 calories, 37% of calories from fat, 4.52 gm fiber, 0.00 mg cholesterol, 170 mg sodium, 12.6 gm fat, 2.02 gm saturated fat, 4.95 gm polyunsaturated fat, 4.07 gm monounsaturated fat.

Crumbly Peaches

3 cups sliced peaches, fresh
 works best
2¼ cups oat bran
½ cup whole wheat flour
¼ cup slivered almonds
2 tablespoons sugar
¼ teaspoon cinnamon
½ cup cholesterol-free margarine

Place the peaches in a square casserole dish. Combine the dry ingredients and then add the margarine, working by hand until crumbly. Spread over the peaches and bake at 375° for 35 minutes or until golden.
 Serves 4.

Per serving: 526 calories, 47% of calories from fat, 12.5 gm fiber, 0.00 mg cholesterol, 308 mg sodium, 30.4 gm fat, 4.33 gm saturated fat, 10.7 gm polyunsaturated fat, 10.6 gm monounsaturated fat.

Old-Fashioned Apple-Raisin Cookies

1⅔ cups old-fashioned
  rolled oats
1¼ cups oat bran
1 cup unbleached all-pur-
  pose flour
¾ cup fine whole wheat
  flour
    •   •   •

½ cup safflower oil
½ cup unsweetened orange
  juice
⅓ cup honey
    •   •   •

¼ teaspoon nutmeg
1 teaspoon cinnamon
⅛ teaspoon ground cloves
½ teaspoon baking powder
    •   •   •

1 cup peeled and sliced apples, pureed in food
  processor
1 cup raisins
½ cup chopped pecans

Combine the rolled oats, oat bran, and flours in a bowl. Add the oil, orange juice, and honey. Stir until thoroughly blended. Add the spices and baking powder. Stir in apples, raisins, and pecans. Drop by tablespoons onto a cookie sheet and bake at 350° for 12 to 15 minutes.

Makes 24 cookies.

Per serving: 172 calories, 42% of calories from fat, 2.29 gm fiber, 0.00 mg cholesterol, 8.23 mg sodium, 8.46 gm fat, 0.94 gm saturated fat, 2.48 gm polyunsaturated fat, 3.85 gm monounsaturated fat.

Apricot-Walnut Cookies

½ cup safflower oil
½ cup honey
½ cup unsweetened orange
　juice
4 egg whites
½ teaspoon vanilla extract

　　•　　•　　•

1¼ cups fine whole wheat
　flour
1 teaspoon baking powder
½ teaspoon cinnamon
1¼ cups oat bran
3 cups old-fashioned rolled
　oats

　　•　　•　　•

½ cup finely chopped dried
　apricots
½ cup finely chopped wal-
　nuts
½ teaspoon grated orange
　rind

Beat together the oil, honey, orange juice, egg whites, and vanilla. Stir in the flour, baking powder, cinnamon, oat bran, and rolled oats. Mix together until well-blended. Stir in the dried apricots, walnuts, and orange rind. Drop by rounded tablespoons onto cookie sheets and bake at 350° for 12 to 15 minutes.

Makes 24 cookies.

Per serving: 166 calories, 37% of calories from fat, 1.87 gm fiber, 0.00 mg cholesterol, 23.5 mg sodium, 7.36 gm fat, 0.83 gm saturated fat, 2.69 gm polyunsaturated fat, 2.32 gm monounsaturated fat.

Cranberry-Orange Bar Cookies

1 cup crushed or chopped
  cranberries
2 oranges, ground with
  skins
½ cup crushed un-
  sweetened pineapple
1 cup dark or light brown
  sugar
1⅓ cups cholesterol-free
  margarine
4 egg whites
1 teaspoon vanilla extract
4 cups whole wheat flour
4 cups oat bran
4 teaspoons baking powder
2 teaspoons baking soda

Combine all of the ingredients and mix well. Press into an 11 x 7-inch pan. Bake at 350° for 12 to 15 minutes or until firm. Cut into bars while hot, then remove from the pan when cool.
  Serves 12.

Per serving: 499 calories, 39% of calories from fat, 9.77 gm fiber, 0.00 mg cholesterol, 545 mg sodium, 23.0 gm fat, 3.60 gm saturated fat, 8.72 gm polyunsaturated fat, 7.18 gm monounsaturated fat.

Oat Bran Cookies

½ cup old-fashioned rolled
  oats for toasting

  •   •   •

½ cup safflower oil
½ cup honey
3 egg whites
2 teaspoons vanilla extract

Place ½ cup of old-fashioned rolled oats on a cookie sheet and bake at 300° for approximately 5 minutes until brown. Cream together the oil and honey. Beat in the egg whites, vanilla, and orange juice. Stir in the toasted oats and remaining ingredients, and mix well. Drop by teaspoons onto greased baking sheets about 1 inch apart.

½ cup unsweetened orange
  juice

.   .   .

½ teaspoon cinnamon
¼ teaspoon nutmeg
1 cup wheat germ
1½ cups oat bran
1 cup raisins
1 cup old-fashioned rolled
  oats
½ cup fine whole wheat
  pastry flour

Bake at 350° for 10 to 12 minutes. Turn out onto wire racks to cool.
Makes 48 cookies.

Per serving: 72.1 calories, 34% of calories from fat, 1.01 gm fiber, 0.00 mg cholesterol, 3.78 mg sodium, 2.92 gm fat, 0.38 gm saturated fat, 1.01 gm polyunsaturated fat, 1.02 gm monounsaturated fat.

Oatmeal Cookies

2 cups old-fashioned oats,
  uncooked
½ cup oat bran
¾ teaspoon baking soda
1 tablespoon vegetable oil
½ cup egg substitute
1 teaspoon vanilla extract
1 cup unsweetened crushed
  pineapple, undrained
1 medium banana, mashed
½ cup raisins
¼ teaspoon cinnamon
⅛ teaspoon nutmeg

Combine all of the ingredients with a spoon. Drop by teaspoonfuls onto a greased cookie sheet. Bake at 350° for 12 minutes.
Makes approximately 42 cookies.

Per serving: 40.6 calories, 19% of calories from fat, 0.70 gm fiber, 0.04 mg cholesterol, 20.3 mg sodium, 0.95 gm fat, 0.08 gm saturated fat, 0.18 gm polyunsaturated fat, 0.17 gm monounsaturated fat.

Old-Fashioned Sorghum Cookies

½ cup sorghum
1 cup cholesterol-free margarine
4 egg whites
1 teaspoon vanilla extract
   •   •   •

2 cups whole wheat flour
1½ cups oat bran
¼ cup wheat germ
2 teaspoons baking soda
1 teaspoon cinnamon
   •   •   •

⅔ cup chopped pecans
Pecan halves
⅔ cup finely chopped mixed
   dried fruits

Beat the sorghum and margarine until fluffy in a mixing bowl. Add the egg whites and vanilla. Stir together the flour, oat bran, wheat germ, soda, and cinnamon in a separate bowl. Stir into the beaten mixture, blending well. Stir in the pecans and dried fruits. With an ice cream scoop, place heaping rounds on a cookie sheet. Place a pecan half in the center of each cookie and press down. Bake at 350° for 10 to 12 minutes. Cool slightly before removing, for these are soft until cooled.
   Makes approximately 5 dozen cookies.

Per serving: 69.6 calories, 50% of calories from fat, 1.08 gm fiber, 0.00 mg cholesterol, 72.2 mg sodium, 4.13 gm fat, 0.61 gm saturated fat, 1.54 gm polyunsaturated fat, 1.59 gm monounsaturated fat.

Peanut Butter-Chocolate Chip Cookies

4 egg whites
½ cup brown sugar
1¼ cups chunky peanut butter
½ cup cholesterol-free margarine
½ cup unsweetened orange
   juice

Combine the egg whites, brown sugar, peanut butter, margarine, orange juice, and vanilla in a large bowl. In a separate bowl, combine the flour, oats, and oat bran. Mix well. Add the dry ingredients to the wet ingredients. Add chocolate bits and stir well. Spoon onto cookie sheets and flatten by hand. Bake at 350° for 10 to 12 minutes.

1 teaspoon vanilla extract
2 teaspoons baking soda
1 cup all-purpose flour
3 cups quick-cooking oats
¾ cup oat bran
½ cup semi-sweet chocolate
   bits

Cool slightly before removing from the cookie sheet.
   Makes 4 dozen cookies.

Per serving: 109 calories, 50% of calories from fat, 1.09 gm fiber, 0.00 mg cholesterol, 95.9 mg sodium, 6.45 gm fat, 1.28 gm saturated fat, 1.85 gm polyunsaturated fat, 2.32 gm monounsaturated fat.

Peanut Butter and Jelly Cookies

¼ cup brown sugar
½ cup cholesterol-free margarine
2 egg whites
½ cup unhydrogenated pea-
   nut butter
   .   .

1¼ cups oat bran
1 cup unbleached all-pur-
   pose flour
½ teaspoon baking powder
½ teaspoon baking soda
   .   .   .

⅓ cup pure unsweetened
   grape jam

Cream the brown sugar, margarine, egg whites, and peanut butter together. Stir in the oat bran, flour, baking powder, and baking soda. Roll into balls approximately 1 inch in diameter. Make a thumb print indention in the center of the cookie. Fill the indention with a small amount of jelly. Bake at 350° for 12 to 15 minutes. Cool for 5 minutes before removing from the cookie sheet.
   Makes 36 cookies.

Per serving: 74.2 calories, 53% of calories from fat, 0.95 gm fiber, 0.00 mg cholesterol, 70.1 mg sodium, 4.60 gm fat, 0.74 gm saturated fat, 1.64 gm polyunsaturated fat, 1.78 gm monounsaturated fat.

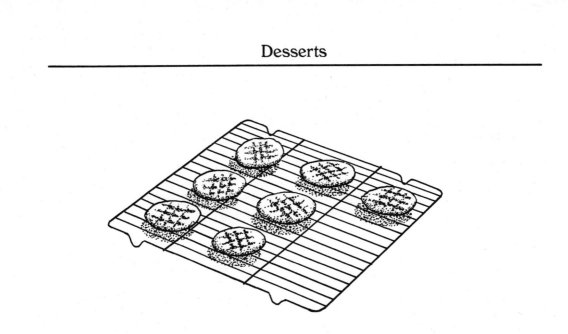

Spicy Peanut Butter Cookies

8 ounces unhydrogenated
  peanut butter
¼ cup cholesterol-free margarine
¼ cup honey

½ cup oat bran
1 cup finely ground whole
  wheat flour
¼ cup unsweetened orange
  juice
¼ teaspoon finely grated orange rind
¼ teaspoon nutmeg
¼ teaspoon cinnamon
¼ teaspoon ground cloves

Cream the peanut butter, margarine, and honey together. Stir in the oat bran, flour, orange juice, orange rind and spices. Roll into 1 inch balls. Place on a cookie sheet and flatten each cookie with a fork. Bake at 350° for 12 to 15 minutes.
  Makes 40 cookies.

Per serving: 64.6 calories, 54% of calories from fat, 1.23 gm fiber, 0.00 mg cholesterol, 42.1 mg sodium, 4.18 gm fat, 0.69 gm saturated fat, 1.36 gm polyunsaturated fat, 1.81 gm monounsaturated fat.

at Bran Cookies

eam the margarine and brown sugar with an
ectric mixer at medium speed until light and
ffy. Add the egg whites, orange juice, and va-
a. Mix until well blended. Combine the flour,
t bran, oats, baking powder, baking soda, and
namon in a separate bowl. Add to the mar-
ine mixture and beat at medium speed until
combined. With a wooden spoon, stir in the
ins and walnuts. Drop the batter by table-
ons onto baking sheets. Bake at 350° for 12
utes.

akes 24 cookies.

*r serving: 109 calories, 45% of calories from fat, 0.93 gm
0.00 mg cholesterol, 85.3 mg sodium, 5.75 gm fat, 0.81
aturated fat, 2.62 gm polyunsaturated fat, 1.70 gm
ounsaturated fat.*

MISCELLANEOUS

Oat Bran Pretzels

1 ¼-ounce package active
  dry yeast
1½ cups warm water (105°
  to 115° F.)
1 cup oat bran
2½ cups all-purpose flour
1 tablespoon sugar
1 egg white

Combine the dry yeast and warm water in a large bowl, stirring until dissolved. Add the oat bran and let the mixture stand for 5 minutes. Combine the flour and sugar in a medium bowl. Using a wooden spoon, stir the flour into the bran mixture until well-combined. Turn onto a floured surface and knead until smooth. Cover and let the dough stand for 5 to 10 minutes.

Divide the dough into 12 pieces and roll each into a 13-inch rope. Form into pretzel shapes and place on a greased cookie sheet. Brush lightly with the egg white. Bake at 425° for 12 to 15 minutes.

Makes 12 pretzels.

Per serving: 124 calories, 5% of calories from fat, 1.75 gm fiber, 0.00 mg cholesterol, 4.68 mg sodium, 0.71 gm fat, 0.04 gm saturated fat, 0.00 gm polyunsaturated fat, 0.00 gm monounsaturated fat.

Crispy Crackers

2 cups quick or regular
  rolled oats
1½ cups all-purpose flour
⅓ cup finely ground pecans
1½ tablespoons brown
  sugar
1 teaspoon salt substitute
⅔ cup water
½ cup safflower oil
6 tablespoons sesame
  seeds

Crush the oats in a food processor. Combine the crushed oats, flour, pecans, brown sugar, and salt substitute in a large bowl. Mix until well blended. Add the water and oil. Blend thoroughly. Divide the dough into 3 balls. Place each ball on a 16" x 12" baking sheet. Roll the dough all the way to the edges. This will be very thin. Sprinkle the dough with sesame seeds. With a pastry wheel or pizza wheel, cut the dough into 2-inch squares or diamonds. Bake at 325° for 30 to 35 minutes or until golden brown. Remove carefully with a spatula. Store in an airtight container for up to a month. The crackers may also be frozen.

Makes 96 crackers.

Per serving: 31.9 calories, 49% of calories from fat, 0.17 gm fiber, 0.00 mg cholesterol, 0.38 mg sodium, 1.81 gm fat, 0.23 gm saturated fat, 0.61 gm polyunsaturated fat, 0.75 gm monounsaturated fat.

Oat Bran Sesame Crackers

1½ cups oat bran
1 cup whole wheat flour
½ cup wheat germ
¼ cup toasted sesame
   seeds
⅓ cup Puritan oil
½ cup sugar-free lemon
   lime soda

Combine the oat bran, flour, wheat germ, and sesame seeds in a bowl. Add the oil and slowly add the lemon lime soda. Form into a stiff ball. Place the ball on a flat greased baking sheet. Roll out until very thin. Cut into rectangles approximately 1 inch x 1½ inch. Bake at 350° for 30 minutes, or until the tops are lightly browned. Separate the crackers and let them stand to dry.
   Makes 90 crackers.

Per serving: 20.7 calories, 48% of calories from fat, 0.48 gm fiber, 0.00 mg cholesterol, 0.38 mg sodium, 1.19 gm fat, 0.16 gm saturated fat, 0.43 gm polyunsaturated fat, 0.43 gm monounsaturated fat.

Granola Treat

4 cups quick or old-fash-
   ioned rolled oats
½ cup oat bran
½ cup chopped nuts
1½ cups apple cider
   •   •   •
½ cup raisins
½ cup diced dried apricots

Combine the oats, oat bran, and nuts. Pour the apple cider into the dry ingredients and mix well. Spread out on jelly-roll pans or baking sheets. Bake at 350° for 30 to 40 minutes or until golden brown and crunchy, stirring occasionally. Stir in the raisins and apricots and cool on the pans. Keep refrigerated in an airtight container.
   Serves 16.

Per serving: 142 calories, 24% of calories from fat, 1.15 gm fiber, 0.00 mg cholesterol, 1.97 mg sodium, 4.07 gm fat, 0.22 gm saturated fat, 1.49 gm polyunsaturated fat, 0.54 gm monounsaturated fat.

Pineapple-Raisin Granola

1 cup old-fashioned rolled oats
1 cup oat bran flake cereal
½ cup wheat germ
1 cup hulled unsalted sunflower seeds
½ cup sesame seeds
½ cup honey
¼ cup safflower oil
½ cup cold water

•   •   •

1 cup chopped almonds

•   •   •

½ cup yellow currants
½ cup dried pineapple bits

Lightly oil a large baking sheet. Combine the oats, oat bran flakes, wheat germ, sunflower seeds, and sesame seeds in a large bowl. Mix well. Combine the honey and oil in a separate bowl. Pour the liquid mixture over the oat mixture and mix well. Slowly add the water and stir until the mixture is crumbly.

Spread the mixture onto a baking sheet. Bake slowly at 225° for 1 hour and 30 minutes, stirring every 30 minutes. Remove from the oven and stir the almonds into the mixture. Bake an additional 30 minutes or until the mixture is crispy. Turn off the oven after 30 minutes and leave the mixture inside until completely cooled. Stir in the currants and pineapple. Store the mixture in an airtight container.

Serves 16.

Per serving: 254 calories, 51% of calories from fat, 2.90 gm fiber, 0.00 mg cholesterol, 2.89 mg sodium, 15.5 gm fat, 1.75 gm saturated fat, 6.33 gm polyunsaturated fat, 5.97 gm monounsaturated fat.

Oat Bran Shaker

½ cup rolled oats
1 tablespoon dried onion
  bits
½ teaspoon minced garlic
¼ teaspoon pepper
¼ teaspoon paprika

Spread the rolled oats on a cookie sheet and bake at 350° for 15 minutes. Combine the baked rolled oats, onion bits, garlic, pepper, and paprika. Mix well. Keep in a jar and use to sprinkle for flavoring meats, vegetables, salads, whatever!

Makes 9 tablespoonfuls.

This is a mix that can be used to sprinkle on top of baked potatoes, fish, vegetables, and so forth for seasoning and adding spice to your life.

Per serving: 16.6 calories, 16% of calories from fat, 0.00 gm fiber, 0.00 mg cholesterol, 0.00 mg sodium, 0.33 gm fat, 0.00 gm saturated fat, 0.00 gm polyunsaturated fat, 0.00 gm monounsaturated fat.

Apple-Cinnamon Oatmeal

4 cups skim milk
Brown sugar substitute
  equivalent to ½ cup
  brown sugar
2 teaspoons cholesterol-
  free margarine
½ teaspoon cinnamon
  •   •   •
¼ cup oat bran
2 cups rolled oats
2 cups peeled and chopped
  apples
1 cup walnuts
1 cup raisins
1 cup wheat germ

Combine the milk, brown sugar substitute, margarine, and cinnamon. Heat until the milk is scalded. Combine the milk mixture with the remaining ingredients in a greased 2-quart casserole. Cover and bake at 350° for 45 minutes or microwave for 10 minutes at full power. Stir several times.

Serves 6.

Per serving: 543 calories, 29% of calories from fat, 4.83 gm fiber, 2.67 mg cholesterol, 112 mg sodium, 18.5 gm fat, 1.93 gm saturated fat, 9.68 gm polyunsaturated fat, 3.66 gm monounsaturated fat.

Apple-Oatmeal Cereal

1 cup skim milk
¼ cup quick or old-fash-
   ioned rolled oats
3 tablespoons oat bran
½ cup unsweetened ap-
   plesauce
1 packet sugar substitute
¼ teaspoon cinnamon
3 drops vanilla extract

Heat the skim milk until hot and steamy but not boiling in a medium saucepan. Add the oats and oat bran. Stir until well-blended. Add the applesauce, sugar substitute, cinnamon, and vanilla. Stir well and serve hot.

Serves 2.

Per serving: 138 calories, 10% of calories from fat, 2.27 gm fiber, 2.00 mg cholesterol, 64.3 mg sodium, 1.65 gm fat, 0.15 gm saturated fat, 0.02 gm polyunsaturated fat, 0.06 gm monounsaturated fat.

Grandma's Old-Fashioned Maple Oatmeal

2½ cups water
2 cups oatmeal
¼ cup oat bran
2 tablespoons honey
½ teaspoon cinnamon
½ teaspoon maple flavoring
1 5-ounce can evaporated
   skim milk

   •   •   •

3 tablespoons cholesterol-
   free margarine, melted
2 tablespoons brown sugar

Bring the water to a boil. Add the oatmeal and oat bran gradually. Continue stirring. Add the honey, cinnamon, and maple flavoring. Cook for 1 minute. Add the evaporated milk and reheat to boiling. Pour into serving dishes and top with margarine and brown sugar.

Serves 6.

Per serving: 220 calories, 31% of calories from fat, 0.55 gm fiber, 0.95 mg cholesterol, 105 mg sodium, 8.03 gm fat, 1.01 gm saturated fat, 2.46 gm polyunsaturated fat, 2.04 gm monounsaturated fat.

Müesli

1 cup old-fashioned rolled
  oats
¾ cup oat bran
1¼ cups skim milk
¾ cup diced dried apricots
1 tablespoon grated orange
  rind
¼ cup orange juice
⅓ cup wheat germ
¼ cup honey

Combine all of the ingredients in a bowl and blend well. Cover and refrigerate overnight or for 8 hours. Before serving, stir thoroughly. This can be prepared ahead and stored for as long as 24 hours.
Serves 6.

Per serving: 214 calories, 10% of calories from fat, 3.46 gm fiber, 0.83 mg cholesterol, 28.8 mg sodium, 2.65 gm fat, 0.18 gm saturated fat, 0.43 gm polyunsaturated fat, 0.16 gm monounsaturated fat.

Index

Index

Index